CAMBRIDGE PRIMARY
Mathematics

Learner's Book

6

Emma Low

CAMBRIDGE
UNIVERSITY PRESS

CAMBRIDGE
UNIVERSITY PRESS

University Printing House, Cambridge CB2 8BS, United Kingdom

Cambridge University Press is part of the University of Cambridge.

It furthers the University's mission by disseminating knowledge in the pursuit of education, learning and research at the highest international levels of excellence.

Information on this title: education.cambridge.org

© Cambridge University Press 2014

First published 2014
9th printing 2016

Printed in India by Multivista Global Pvt Ltd

A catalogue record for this publication is available from the British Library

ISBN 978-1-107-61859-6 Paperback

Introduction

This *Learner's Book* is a supplementary resource that consolidates and reinforces mathematical learning alongside the *Cambridge Primary Mathematics Teacher's Resource 6* (9781107694361). It provides introductory investigations (Let's investigate) to encourage the application of mathematical knowledge, and numerous questions and activities to develop problem-solving skills.

Ideally, a session should be taught using the appropriate *Core activity* in the *Teacher's Resource 6*. The associated content in the *Learner's Book 6* can then be used for formative assessment at the end of a session, for homework or used for support in learning new vocabulary. There is generally a double page corresponding to each *Core activity* in the *Teacher's Resource 6* printed book. The *Core activity* that the page relates to is indicated at the bottom of the page.

Hints and tips are provided throughout to support the learners. They will appear as follows:

Write a list of number pairs to help you

Please note that the *Learner's Book* on its own does **not** cover all of the Cambridge Primary mathematics curriculum framework for Stage 6. You need to use it in conjunction with the *Teacher's Resource 6* to ensure full coverage.

This publication is part of the *Cambridge Primary Maths* project. *Cambridge Primary Maths* is an innovative combination of curriculum and resources designed to support teachers and learners to succeed in primary mathematics through best-practice international maths teaching and a problem-solving approach.

Cambridge Primary Maths brings together the world-class Cambridge Primary mathematics curriculum from Cambridge International Examinations, high-quality publishing from Cambridge University Press and expertise in engaging online enrichment materials for the mathematics curriculum from NRICH.

Teachers have access to an online tool that maps resources and links to materials offered through the primary mathematics curriculum, NRICH and Cambridge Primary mathematics textbooks and e-books. These resources include engaging online activities, best-practice guidance and examples of *Cambridge Primary Maths* in action.

The Cambridge curriculum is dedicated to helping schools develop learners who are confident, responsible, reflective, innovative and engaged. It is designed to give learners the skills to problem solve effectively, apply mathematical knowledge and develop a holistic understanding of the subject.

The *Cambridge Primary Maths* textbooks provide best-in-class support for this problem-solving approach, based on pedagogical practice found in successful schools across the world. The engaging NRICH online resources help develop mathematical thinking and problem-solving skills. To get involved visit www.cie.org.uk/cambridgeprimarymaths

The benefits of being part of *Cambridge Primary Maths* are:
- the opportunity to explore a maths curriculum founded on the values of the University of Cambridge and best practice in schools
- access to an innovative package of online and print resources that can help bring the Cambridge Primary mathematics curriculum to life in the classroom.

This series is arranged to ensure that the curriculum is covered whilst allowing teachers to use a flexible approach. The Scheme of Work for Stage 6 has been followed, though not in the same order and there will be some deviations. The components are:
- Teacher's Resource 6
  ISBN: 9781107694361 (printed book and CD-ROM).
- Learner's Book 6
  ISBN: 9781107618596 (printed book)
- Games Book 6
  ISBN: 9781107667815 (printed book and CD-ROM).

For associated NRICH activities, please visit the *Cambridge Primary Maths* project at www.cie.org.uk/cambridgeprimarymaths

Number

Place value

Let's investigate

Raphael has eight digit cards.

Vocabulary

million: equal to one thousand thousands and written as 1 000 000.

1 million = 10 × 10 × 10 × 10 × 10 × 10

He uses the cards to make two four-digit numbers. He uses each card only once.

He finds the difference between his two numbers.

What is the largest difference he can make?

Think about the largest and smallest numbers you can make.

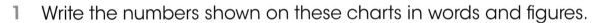

1 Write the numbers shown on these charts in words and figures.

(a)

100 000	200 000	300 000	400 000	500 000	600 000	700 000	800 000	900 000
10 000	20 000	30 000	40 000	50 000	60 000	70 000	80 000	90 000
1000	2000	3000	4000	5000	6000	7000	8000	9000
100	200	300	400	500	600	700	800	900
10	20	30	40	50	60	70	80	90
1	2	3	4	5	6	7	8	9
0.1	0.2	0.3	0.4	0.5	0.6	0.7	0.8	0.9
0.01	0.02	0.03	0.04	0.05	0.06	0.07	0.08	0.09

(b)

100 000	200 000	300 000	400 000	500 000	600 000	700 000	800 000	900 000
10 000	20 000	30 000	40 000	50 000	60 000	70 000	80 000	90 000
1000	2000	3000	4000	5000	6000	7000	8000	9000
100	200	300	400	500	600	700	800	900
10	20	30	40	50	60	70	80	90
1	2	3	4	5	6	7	8	9
0.1	0.2	0.3	0.4	0.5	0.6	0.7	0.8	0.9
0.01	0.02	0.03	0.04	0.05	0.06	0.07	0.08	0.09

(c)

100 000	200 000	300 000	400 000	500 000	600 000	700 000	800 000	900 000
10 000	20 000	30 000	40 000	50 000	60 000	70 000	80 000	90 000
1000	2000	3000	4000	5000	6000	7000	8000	9000
100	200	300	400	500	600	700	800	900
10	20	30	40	50	60	70	80	90
1	2	3	4	5	6	7	8	9
0.1	0.2	0.3	0.4	0.5	0.6	0.7	0.8	0.9
0.01	0.02	0.03	0.04	0.05	0.06	0.07	0.08	0.09

2 Write these numbers in figures:

(a) one million

(b) five hundred thousand and five

(c) four hundred and three thousand, and thirty four point six six.

3 Write these numbers in words:

(a) 345 678   (b) 537 914   (c) 158 035.4   (d) 303 033.03

4 (a) Write half a million in figures.

(b) Add 10 to half a million. Write your answer in words and figures.

5 What value does the digit 7 have in these numbers?

(a) 670 346.5   (b) 702 138   (c) 606 456.7   (b) 234 560.07

6 Write these numbers in words and figures.

(a) 200 000 + 6000 + 300 + 2

(b) 900 000 + 90 000 + 900 + 9 + 0.9

(c) 100 000 + 20 000 + 5000 + 600 + 20 + 5 + 0.4 + 0.03

7 Noura has these cards.

(a) What is the largest even number she can make using all the cards.

(b) What is the smallest odd number she can make using all the cards.

Ordering, comparing and rounding numbers

Let's investigate

There are 1187 students in a large city school.

There are 42 classes in the school.

Approximately, how many students are in each class?

Explain to a friend how you made your decision.

Do not attempt to work out an accurate answer.

1   Draw a line 10 centimetres long. Mark 0 and 10 000 at the end points.

0   10 000

Estimate the positions of the following numbers.
Mark each one with an arrow and its letter:
6000 marked A
3500 marked B
9050 marked C

2   Round these numbers to the nearest hundred.
    (a) 45 678   (b) 24 055   (c) 50 505

3   Round these numbers to the nearest thousand.
    (a) 147 950   (b) 65 507   (c) 157 846

4   Order the following sets of numbers from smallest to largest.
    (a) 54 754   55 475   55 547   54 775   55 447
    (b) 45 054   45 540   45 504   45 045   45 500
    (c) 456 065   450 566   455 656   456 565   450 666
    Use any of the numbers in part (c) to complete these inequalities.

    [?] < [?]   [?] > [?]

4

5 The table shows the heights of mountain summits in five different continents.

Mountain summit	Continent	Height (in metres)
Kilimanjaro	Africa	5895
Everest	Asia	8848
Kosciuszko	Australia	2228
McKinley	North America	6194
Aconcagua	South America	6961

(a) Order the heights starting with the smallest.

(b) Round each height to the nearest hundred metres.

6 Choose one of these numbers to complete each inequality.

35 055   35 550   35 050   35 005   35 500   35 505

(a) ? > 35 055   (b) 35 500 > ?   (c) ? < 35 505

7 Here is a number sentence.

  ? − 1300 > 6500

Which of these numbers will make the number sentence correct?

4000   5000   6000   7000   8000   9000

8 The table shows the lengths of some rivers in the United Kingdom.

River	Length (to the nearest km)
Dee	113
Severn	354
Thames	346
Trent	297
Wye	215

Write each length:

(a) to the nearest 10 km

(b) to the nearest 100 km.

(c) There is another river which is not on the list. It is 200 km to the nearest 100 km and 150 km to the nearest 10 km. What are the possible lengths of this river?

Multiples and factors

Let's investigate

The sequence below uses the numbers 1 to 4 so that each number is either a factor or a multiple of the previous number.

Each number is used once only.

Find a similar sequence that uses the numbers 1 to 6.

Use cards that can be easily moved around.

1 Which of these numbers are multiples of 8?

   18   24   48   56   68   72

2 Which of these numbers are factors of 30?

   4   5   6   10   20   60

3 Use each of the digits 5, 6, 7 and 8 once to make a total that is a multiple of 5.

   | ? | ? | + | ? | ? |

4 Find all the factors of:
   (a) 24   (b) 32   (c) 25.

5 My age this year is a multiple of 8.
   My age next year is a multiple of 7.
   How old am I?

factor: a whole number that divides exactly into another number. For example, 1, 2, 3 and 6 are the factors of 6.

$1 \times 6 = 6 \quad 2 \times 3 = 6$

factor factor factor factor

multiple: a number that can be divided exactly by another number is a multiple of that number. Start at 0 and count up in steps of the same size and you will find numbers that are multiples of the step size. For example,

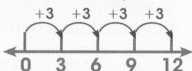

3, 6, 9, 12 . . . are multiples of 3.

6 Draw a sorting diagram like the one shown.
Write one number in each section of the diagram.

	less than 1000	not less than 1000
multiples of 25		
not multiples of 25		

7 Draw the Venn diagram below. Write the numbers 8, 9, 10, 11, 12 and 13 in the correct places on your Venn diagram.

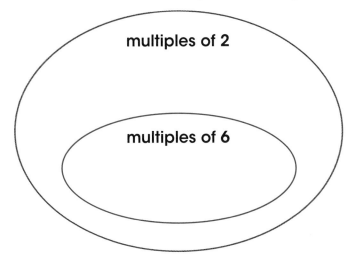

multiples of 2

multiples of 6

8 Use each of the digits 2, 3, 4, 5, 6 and 7 only once to make three two-digit multiples of 3.

?	?		?	?		?	?

9 Here are four labels.

even   multiples of 3   not even   not multiples of 3

Draw the Carroll diagram below and add the labels.

	6 24	16 22
	15 27	17 7

Odd and even numbers

Let's investigate

You need 13 counters and a 5 by 5 grid.

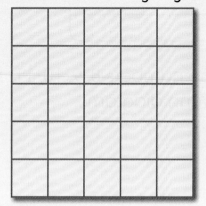

- Place 13 counters on the grid so that there is an odd number of counters in each row, column and on both diagonals. Only one counter can be placed in each cell.
- Place 10 counters on the grid so that there is an even number of counters in each row, column and on both diagonals. Only one counter can be placed in each cell.

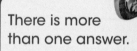

There is more than one answer.

1 Which of these numbers are even?

   9   11   26   33   57   187   2002

   Explain to a partner how you know.

2 Andre makes a three-digit number.
   All the digits are odd.
   The sum of the digits is 7.
   What could Andre's number be?

3 Ollie makes a three-digit number using the digits 2, 3 and 6.
   His number is odd.
   The hundreds digit is greater than 2.
   What could Ollie's number be?

4   Sara makes a four-digit even number.
    The sum of the digits is 4.
    The thousands digit and the units digit are the same.
    The hundreds digit and the tens digit are the same.
    The hundreds digit is 0.
    What is Sara's number?

5   Copy the Carroll diagram for sorting numbers.
    Write these numbers in the diagram:
    27   235   7004   43   660

	odd	not odd
three-digit number		
not a three-digit number		

6   Three different numbers add up to 50.

    | ? | + | ? | + | ? | = 50

    The numbers are all even.
    Each number is greater than 10.
    What could the numbers be?

7   Erik has a set of number cards from 1 to 20.
    He picks four different cards.

    Exactly three of his cards are multiples of 5.
    Exactly three of his cards are even numbers.
    All four of the numbers add up to less than 40.
    What cards could Erik pick?

8   Which number satisfies all of these conditions:
    it is a multiple of 25
    it is even
    it is greater than 550 but less than 700
    it is not 600.

Prime numbers

Let's investigate

Look at this statement.

> Every even number greater than 2 is the sum of two prime numbers.

Here are two examples:

$6 = 3 + 3$ (3 is a prime number)

$12 = 5 + 7$ (5 and 7 are prime numbers)

- Check if the statement is true for all the even numbers to 30.

- Can you find an even number that does not satisfy the rule? Try some numbers greater than 30.

Vocabulary

prime number: a prime number has exactly two different factors; itself and 1.

NOTE: 1 is **not** a prime number. It has only one factor (1).

Examples of prime numbers: 2, 3, 5, 7, 11 …

1 List all the prime numbers between 10 and 20.

2 Identify these prime numbers from the clues.
   (a) It is less than 30.
       The sum of its digits is 8.
   (b) It is between 30 and 60.
       The sum of its digits is 10.

3 Copy and complete these number sentence by placing a prime number in each box.

   | ? | × | ? | × | ? | = 30 |

   | ? | × | ? | × | ? | = 50 |

   | ? | × | ? | × | ? | = 70 |

4 Identify the prime numbers represented by **?** and **?** .

   (a) $?^2 = 49$

   (b) $? + 1 = 2 \times 9$

   (c) $? + 2 = 5^2$

   (d) $? + ? = 20$

Multiplying and dividing by 10, 100 and 1000

Let's investigate

Cheng is thinking of a number.
What number is Cheng thinking of?

I multiply my number by 100, then divide by 10, then multiply by 1000. My answer is one hundred and seventy thousand.

1   Copy and complete this set of missing numbers.

$25 \times 100 = \boxed{?}$ $\boxed{?} \div 100 = 250$

$\boxed{?} \times 10 = 2500$ $250 \div 10 = \boxed{?}$

2   What is the missing number?

$100 \times 10 = 10\,000 \div \boxed{?}$

3   A decagon has 10 sides.

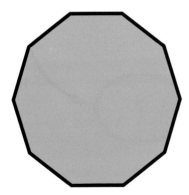

What is the perimeter of a regular decagon with sides 17 centimetres long?

4   Milly says, "Every multiple of 1000 is divisible by 100."
Is she right?
Explain your answer.

For more questions, turn the page ...

5 Find the missing digits. Copy and complete each number sentence.

| ? | ? | ? | × 10 = 5680 |

| ? | ? | ? | ? | ? | = 1000 × 32 |

| 5 | 6 | 0 | ? | ÷ 10 = | ? | 6 | 0 |

| 4 | ? | ? | ? | ? | ÷ 1000 = | ? | 5 |

6 Here are four numbers.

55.5   555   5550   55 500

Which of these numbers is 100 times smaller than 555 000?

7 Copy the diagrams and write in the missing numbers.

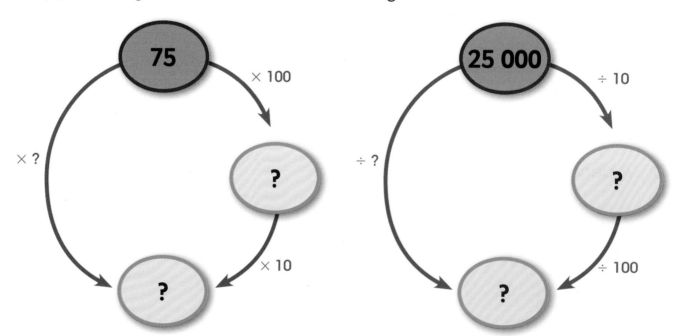

Vocabulary

near multiple of 10: a number either side of a multiple of 10. For example, 20 is a multiple of 10, so 19 and 21 are near multiples of 10.

Let's investigate

Find different ways of completing this calculation.

$$\boxed{?} \times \boxed{?} \times \boxed{?} = 24$$

1   Use the given fact to derive a new fact and then explain your method.
    Copy and complete the table, the first one has been done for you.

	Fact	Derived fact	Method
(a)	$7 \times 9 = 63$	$7 \times 18 = 126$	18 is double 9 so double the answer
(b)	$7 \times 3 = 21$	$70 \times 3 =$	
(c)	$5 \times 7 = 35$	$50 \times 70 =$	
(d)	$6 \times 8 = 48$	$6 \times 16 =$	
(e)	$8 \times 13 = 104$	$4 \times 13 =$	
(f)	$6 \times 7 = 42$	$6 \times 70 =$	
(g)	$5 \times 9 = 45$	$5 \times 91 =$	
(h)	$6 \times 9 = 54$	$6 \times 89 =$	
(i)	$4 \times 7 = 28$	$39 \times 7 =$	
(j)	$3 \times 9 = 27$	$30 \times 91 =$	

2   Use table facts to help you work out the following:

    (a) 30×70 (b) 50×9 (c) 20×6

    (d) 50×80 (e) 8×90 (f) 70×60

3   Work out the following using a mental strategy:

    (a) 29×6 (b) 41×5 (c) 19×7

    (d) 21×8 (e) 49×6 (f) 51×4

Explain to your partner how you worked out the answers.

Addition of decimals

Let's investigate

Arrange the numbers 0.1, 0.2, 0.3, 0.4, 0.5 and 0.6 in the circles so the sum along each side of the triangle is 1.2.

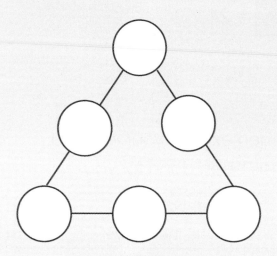

Try using numbers on cards or small pieces of paper, that you can move around.

1   The answers to the following questions are in the grid.
    Find which answer goes with which question.
    Which number is not one of the answers?

8.28	4.3	2.05
7.8	5.41	12.18
13.95	4.98	12.21

(a) 4.61 + 0.8   (b) 0.45 + 1.6   (c) 3.7 + 4.58   (d) 6.1 + 7.85

(e) 4.3 + 0.68   (f) 7.5 + 4.68   (g) 4.25 + 7.96   (h) 3.45 + 0.85

2   Kiki has two pieces of rope. One piece is 93.7 metres long and the other piece is 125.9 metres long. What is the total length of her rope?

3   Find the sum of all the numbers less than 5.5 in this list.
    5.05   5.55   5.15   5.5

4 A shop has these items for sale.

Coffee maker	$129.95
Toaster	$30.75
Can opener	$14.25
Ice cream maker	$26.80

Darius buys an ice cream maker and a coffee maker. How much does he spend altogether?

5 Use the digits 3, 5 and 6 only to complete these calculations. You can use each digit more than once.

| ? | ? | · | ? | + | ? | ? | · | ? | = 100 |

6 Here are six number cards:

0.3 0.4 0.6 0.7 1 1

Use each card once to complete these two calculations:

? + ? = ?

? + ? = ?

7 Choose one number from each box to make a total of 10. Write down the number sentence.

| 1.5 2.5 | | 2 | | 1.5 2.5 |
| 3.5 4.5 | + | 4 | + | 3.5 4.5 | = 10

8   Add together all the numbers greater than 0.7, in the following list.
    Check your answer by adding the numbers together in a different order.

    0.5   11.2   0.8   0.38   0.09   0.74   2.54

9   Here are ten number cards:

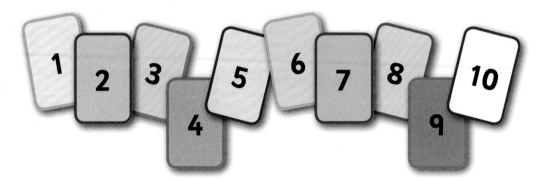

    Divide the cards into five pairs so that one pair adds up to 6, one pair
    adds up to 7, one pair to 9, one pair to 16 and one pair to 17.

10 Use each of the digits 2, 4, 6 and 7 to make this calculation correct:

    $\boxed{?}\,.\,\boxed{?} + \boxed{?}\,.\,\boxed{?} = 10$

11 Petra buys two shirts. One costs $14.75 and the other $21.05.
    What is the total cost of the two shirts?

Division (1)

Let's investigate

Abdul was asked how old he was.

If my age is divided by 2 or 3 or 4 there is 1 left over. If my age is divided by 7 there is no remainder.

How old is Abdul?

List the multiples of 7.

1   Vincent wants to put 75 photographs in an album.
    A full page holds 6 photographs. What is the smallest
    number of pages Vincent uses?

2   Which number on the grid can be
    divided by 8 with a remainder of 1?

67	72	51
42	73	64
60	20	69

3   Complete these calculations:
    (a) 78 ÷ 4   (b) 68 ÷ 7   (c) 98 ÷ 6

4   Copy the grid. Shade the squares
    that have a remainder in the
    answer.
    What letter have you made?

41 ÷ 4	47 ÷ 9	48 ÷ 5
14 ÷ 4	25 ÷ 5	31 ÷ 3
55 ÷ 6	27 ÷ 6	50 ÷ 7
34 ÷ 7	48 ÷ 6	54 ÷ 9
60 ÷ 8	54 ÷ 6	49 ÷ 7

5   Complete these calculations:
    (a) 132 ÷ 6   (b) 146 ÷ 9
    (c) 147 ÷ 2   (d) 107 ÷ 4
    (e) 156 ÷ 8   (f) 148 ÷ 9

Number sequences

Let's investigate

Choose different starting numbers to make sequences that have a rule 'add 5'.

Is it possible to make a sequence where the rule is 'add 5' and the terms are:

- multiples of 5?
- multiples of 10?
- all odd?
- include 24 and 39?
- are not whole numbers?

> You will need to try different starting numbers.

1 Here is the beginning of a sequence of numbers:

8, 16, 24, 32, 40 …

The sequence continues in the same way.

Will 88 be in the sequence? Explain how you know.

2 A sequence starts at 200 and 30 is subtracted each time.

200, 170, 140 …

What are the first two numbers in the sequence that are less than zero?

Vocabulary

sequence: an ordered set of numbers, shapes or other mathematical objects arranged according to a rule. For example, 3, 6, 9, 12, 15 … 1, 4, 9, 16, 25 … □ ○ △ □ ○ △ □

step: the 'jump size'. For example, in the sequence

60 ⌣110 ⌣160 ⌣210
  +50   +50   +50

the step is '+50'.

term: one of the numbers in a sequence.

rule: a rule tells you how things or numbers are connected. For example, the numbers 3, 7, 11, 15, 19 … are connected by the rule 'add 4 to the previous number'.

3 Fatima makes a sequence of five numbers.

The first number is 2.

The last number is 14.

Her rule is, add the same number each time.

What are the missing numbers?

| 2 | ? | ? | ? | 14 |

4 Copy and complete these sequences. (The step size is constant in each sequence.)

(a) 0.6 0.9 ? ? ?

(b) ? $\frac{5}{8}$ $\frac{7}{8}$ $1\frac{1}{8}$?

(c) −7 −5 ? ? ?

(d) ? $1\frac{1}{3}$ $2\frac{2}{3}$ 4 ?

(e) 0.61 0.72 ? ? ?

5 Copy the table and write down the next five terms in these sequences.

	Rule	First term	Next five terms
a	add 4	3	
b	subtract 9	60	
c	multiply by 2	2	
d	divide by 2	128	

6 Copy these sequences and write down the next five terms.

(a) −1 −3 −5 −7 ...   (b) 5 0 −5 −10 ...   (c) 11 5 −1 −7 ...

7 The first term and the rule of the sequence are given.

Write down the next four terms in the sequence:

(a) first term 8   rule: multiply by 2 and add 1

(b) first term 4   rule: subtract 1, then multiply by 2

(c) first term 400   rule: halve the term.

Measure

Measuring length

Let's investigate

Nicola needs to put up bunting around a whole room for a party. The room is 4 m long and 3 m wide. She has lots of 70 cm lengths of bunting. Every time she ties two pieces together she needs to use 50 mm of each piece of string for the knot. How many pieces of 70 cm long bunting does she need to go right around the room?

First work out the perimeter of the room. Choose to do the calculation in mm, cm or m and make all the measurements have the same unit. You could take, or imagine, three or four pieces of string and tie them together to better understand the problem.

Vocabulary

millimetre (mm): a unit for measuring length.

centimetre (cm): a unit for measuring length. There are 10 mm in 1 cm.

metre (m): a unit for measuring length. There are 100 cm in 1 m.

kilometre (km): a unit for measuring length. There are 1000 m in 1 km.

1   Eric has lost his umbrella. At the Lost Property Office he looks at the list of umbrellas that have been handed in. The person who has filled in the Lost Property log seems to have confused the units of length.

Object	Date Handed in	Colour	Length
umbrella	12 September	Black	218 m
umbrella	25 October	Blue (with flowers)	84.9 m
umbrella	26 October	Red	895 cm
umbrella	5 November	Black	97.2 mm
umbrella	19 November	Pink	527 cm
umbrella	20 November	Silver	1.05 cm

(a) Copy the last column of the table. Correct the sizes of the objects so that they have realistic units, keep the numbers the same.

(b) Write the realistic measurements of the lost property in order of size, from shortest to longest.

(c) Eric's umbrella is approximately 90 cm long. Which of the listed umbrella lengths rounds to 90 cm to the nearest ten centimetres?

2 Estimate the length of each line in centimetres, then measure them to the nearest millimetre.

(a)

(b)

(c)

(d)

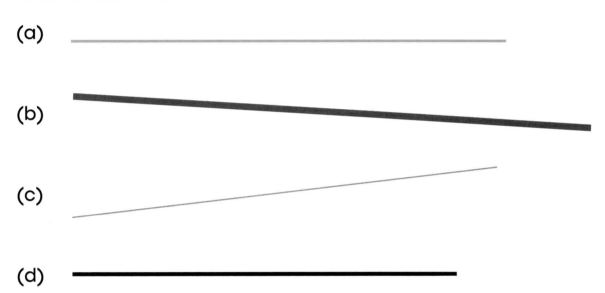

For lines (e) and (f), work with a partner. Make a copy of the length of the line using string and then measure the string with a ruler.

(e)

(f)

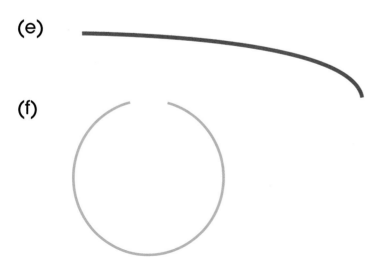

Drawing length

1. Accurately draw straight lines that measure:

   (a) 9.6 cm

   (b) 122 mm

   (c) 0.129 m

   (d) 5.1 cm

   (e) 26 mm

   (f) 0.088 m

   - Your pencil should be sharp.
   - Check the scale on your ruler. If necessary convert the length into the units shown on your ruler.
   - Find '0' and the point on the scale you need to make the correct length before starting to draw the line.

2. Curves and patterns, such as those below, can be made by careful measuring and drawing straight lines. Use your ruler to check that all the lines drawn on the designs are straight.

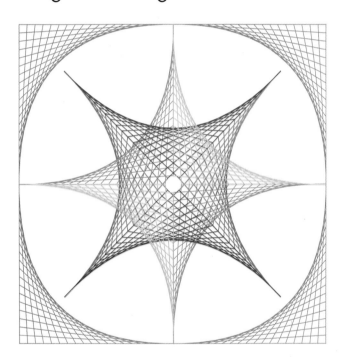
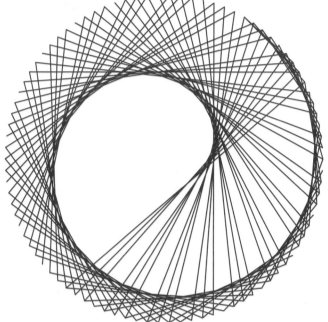

They were made by starting like this:

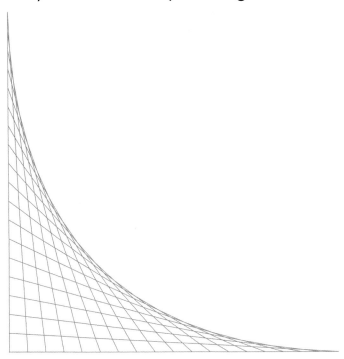

or this:

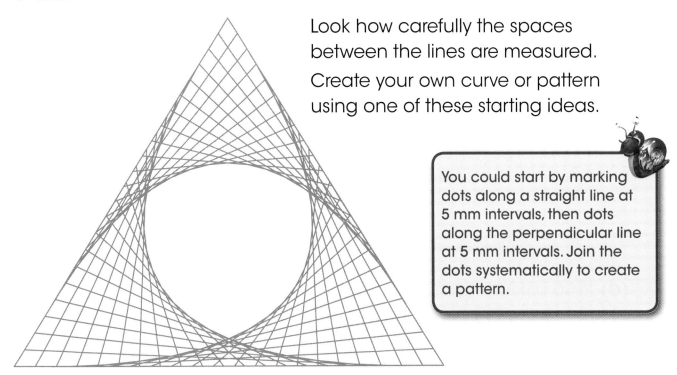

Look how carefully the spaces between the lines are measured.

Create your own curve or pattern using one of these starting ideas.

You could start by marking dots along a straight line at 5 mm intervals, then dots along the perpendicular line at 5 mm intervals. Join the dots systematically to create a pattern.

Telling the time and timetables

Let's investigate

Dylan has a recorded a song which he listens to over and over again. The song is three minutes and 45 seconds long. When the song stops there is a 20 second silent gap before the song starts again.

> You could work out the times that the song will start playing between one o'clock and half past one.

He starts the song playing at one o'clock.

Is the song playing at half past one or is it the silent gap?

1 These children are talking about what time they arrived at a party one afternoon.

I arrived at quarter to three this afternoon.

JASON

I got here at 15:45.

KYLE

I was at the party from twenty past two.

LINA

I arrived at 2:40 pm.

MIA

I got here at 12 minutes to three.

NAOMI

I was at the party from 14:50.

OMAR

(a) Who arrived first, second, third, fourth, fifth and sixth?

The clock on the wall at the party showed this time:

(b) How long had each child been at the party?

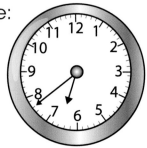

2 The children are all attending a holiday sports club.
   This is a timetable of the activities.

	Time	Sport	Venue
Monday	10:00 – 11:35	Football	Outside Pitch 1
	11:00 – 12:00	Street Dance	Sports Hall 1
	13:30 – 14:40	Tennis	Tennis Court
	14:00 – 15:30	Gymnastics	Sports Hall 2
Tuesday	10:15 – 11:30	Trampoline	Sports Hall 1
	11:00 – 11:50	Swimming	Teaching Pool
	12:00 – 14:00	Cricket	Outside Pitch 1
	15:20 – 16:45	Rugby	Outside Pitch 2
Wednesday	09:35 – 11:00	Creative Dance	Sports Hall 1
	10:45 – 12:00	Trampoline	Sports Hall 2
	12:20 – 14:00	Basketball	Sports Hall 1
	13:10 – 14:45	Football	Outside Pitch 1
Thursday	09:50 – 11:00	Tennis	Tennis Court
	10:30 – 11:55	Rugby	Outside Pitch 2
	13:15 – 14:15	Street Dance	Sports Hall 1
	15:30 – 17:20	Badminton	Sports Hall 2
Friday	09:45 – 11:45	Cricket	Outside Pitch 1
	10:30 – 11:55	Creative Dance	Sports Hall 1
	12:10 – 14:00	Badminton	Sports Hall 2
	13:40 – 14:30	Swimming	Teaching Pool

Plan sports sessions for each child, according to what they like to do.

(a) Jason would like to do basketball, football, cricket and swimming.

(b) Kyle would like to do football, street dance, badminton and cricket.

(c) Lina would like to do tennis, gymnastics, creative dance and trampoline.

(d) Mia would like to do swimming, creative dance, trampoline, and cricket.

(e) Naomi would like to do badminton, football, street dance and
     gymnastics.

(f) Omar would like to do swimming, football, street dance, tennis,
     badminton, cricket, gymnastics and rugby.

(g) How long will Omar spend doing sports during the holiday sports week?

Time intervals and calendars

Let's investigate

I have been alive for 525 600 minutes.

Is this likely to be true? Why?

You could use a calculator to convert the time into hours, days and then years. Use your knowledge of people and the world to give your reasoning.

1   Write these sentences and fill in the missing numbers and words.

There are 100 years in a _____.

There are _____ years in a decade.

There are _____ months in one year.

There are _____ days in one week.

There are _____ hours in one day.

There are 60 _____ in one hour.

There are 60 seconds in one _____.

2   (a) Copy and complete the table with equivalent times.

Days	Hours	Minutes	Seconds
1		1440	86 400
2	48		
3			259 200
4			345 600
5		7200	
6	144		518 400
7		10 080	604 800

   (b) Explain how you can use the table to find out how many seconds there are in one week.

3 This is a page from a calendar.

2023						
Monday	**Tuesday**	**Wednesday**	**Thursday**	**Friday**	**Saturday**	**Sunday**
31	1	2	3	4	5	6
7	8	9	10	11	12	13
14	15	16	17	(18)	19	20
21	22	23	24	25	26	27
28	29	30	31			

(a) What months could this calendar be from? Explain how you know.

(b) If the calendar is from the second half of the year, what is the date circled in red?

(c) Imagine the circled date is today's date. How old would each of these people be in years, months and days?

    (i)   Tim – born 11th July 2013

    (ii)   Sharon – born 2nd April 2006

    (iii)   Caroline – born 27th July 1975

    (iv)   Jack – 18th October 1972

    (v)   Stefan – 30th September 1966

Area and perimeter (1)

Vocabulary

Let's investigate

Each of these five tiles is square and has an area of 16 cm². Find a way to arrange them so that the total shape has a perimeter of 40 cm.

> You could use five squares and move them around into different shapes. Work out the length of each side to help you calculate the perimeter.

area: the measurement of a surface, recorded using square units.

perimeter: the distance around the outside of a 2D shape, recorded using units of length.

1   This pattern is made starting with a square that is 2 cm wide, and by drawing squares 2 cm wider than the last. Complete the table to show the visible area of each colour. Visualise or draw the fourth pattern.

First **Second** **Third**

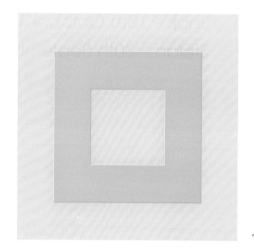

Pattern	Visible yellow area	Visible blue area
First	4 cm²	0 cm²
Second		
Third		
Fourth		

> You could add the yellow area to the blue area to check that it equals the total area of the pattern.

2 On this map each square is 1 km².
   Use the squares to estimate the area of:
   (a) the forest
   (b) the lake
   (c) the whole island (including the forest and lake).

Key			
Island	Forest	Lake	Sea

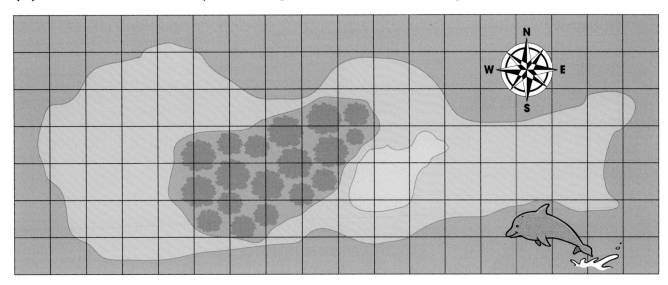

3 For each of these rectangles, measure two sides to the
   nearest millimetre and then calculate the perimeter.

(a)   **(b)**

(c)   **(d)**   **(e)**

Geometry

Polygons and quadrilaterals

Let's investigate

What can you see in the pattern below?

How many:
- squares?
- trapeziums?
- kites?
- right-angles?

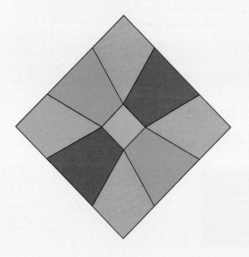

1 These shapes are not polygons. Give at least one reason why each of the shapes is not a polygon.

polygon: a closed 2D shape with three or more straight sides.

quadrilateral: a polygon with exactly four sides.

parallelolgram: a quadrilateral. Both pairs of opposite sides are parallel.

rectangle: a quadrilateral. Both pairs of opposite sides are parallel and all the angles are right angles.

rhombus: a quadrilateral. Both pairs of opposite sides are parallel and all the sides are the same length.

square: a quadrilateral. Both pairs of opposite sides are parallel, all the sides are the same length and all the angles are right angles.

trapezium (also known is some countries as a 'trapezoid'): a quadrilateral. One pair of opposite sides is parallel.

kite: a quadrilateral. Two pairs of adjacent sides are the same length.

(a)

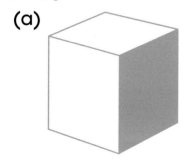

(b)

(c)

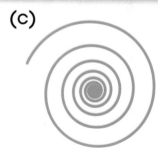

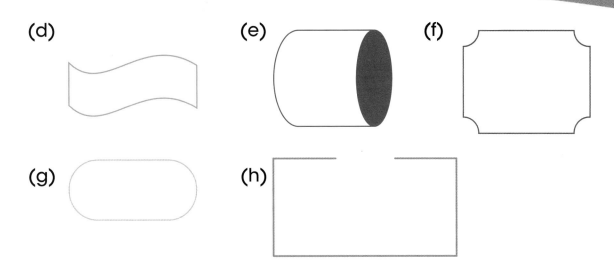

(d)

(e)

(f)

(g)

(h)

2 Copy and complete the table for these shapes.

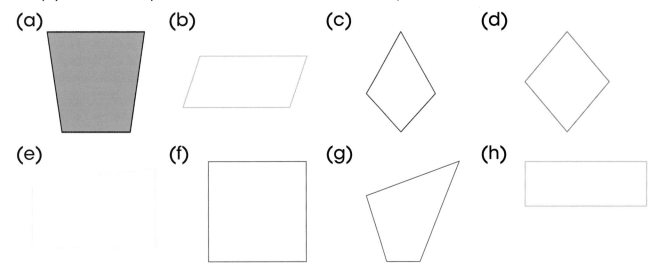

(a)

(b)

(c)

(d)

(e)

(f)

(g)

(h)

	Number of right angles	Number of pairs of parallel sides	Most specific name
(a)			
(b)			
(c)			
(d)			
(e)			
(f)			
(g)			
(h)			

Use the vocabulary list to find the most specific name for each shape.

3 Make your own pattern (see example in **Let's investigate**) using at least three different types of quadrilateral.

3D shapes

Let's investigate

Imagine Kate made a solid octagonal pyramid.
She carefully cut right through the shape with a knife
and looked to see what shape she had made inside.

Which of these shapes could she not have made:

- an octagon
- a triangle
- a rhombus
- a trapezium?

Explain to someone how she could have made each
of the other shapes.

1   Francesca put six shapes
    into a bag. Her friends
    each took at shape at
    random and described
    their shape.

What shape could each child be talking about?

(a)

8 edges and
5 vertices

Nets

Let's investigate

On a six-sided dice the numbers on opposite faces total 7.

Complete the numbers on this net so that each pair
of opposite faces total 7.

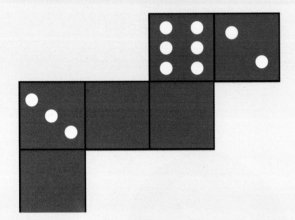

Remember, opposite faces will
not touch when the net is folded,
so cannot touch on the net.

1   Draw a net that could make a 3D shape that would look like this:

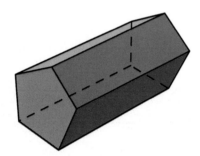

2   Measure the faces of this net. Draw a picture of the 3D shape that
would be made from this net. Label the measurements of
the length, width and height of the shape.

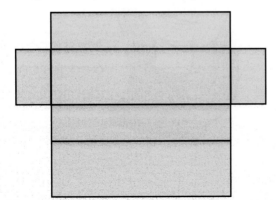

3   Which of the nets would make which 3D shape?
    Match the net to the picture.

(a)

(b)

(c)

(d)

(e)

(f)

(g)

(h)

(i)

(j)

(k)

(l)

(m)

(n)

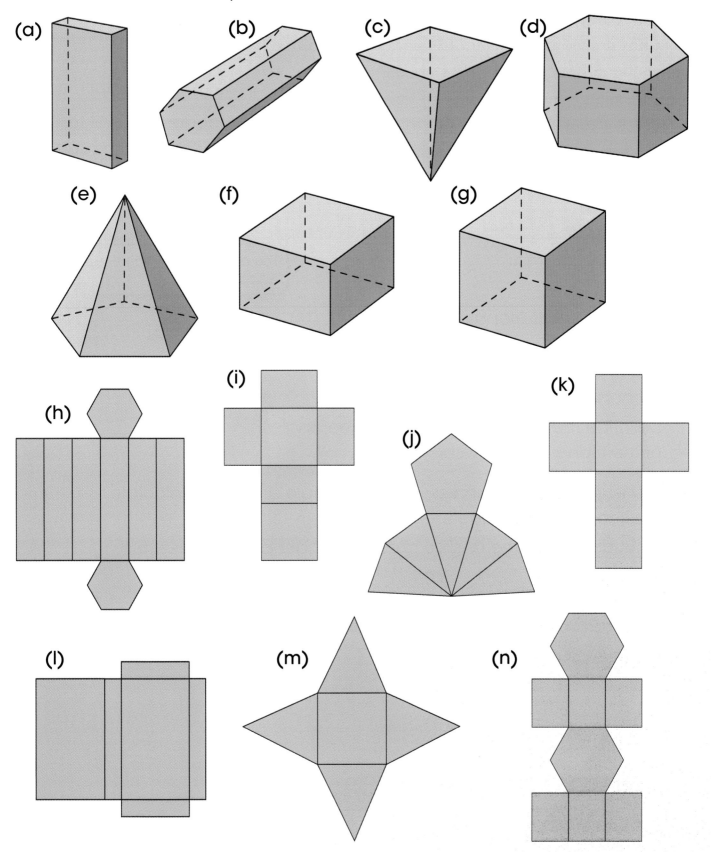

Angles in a triangle

Vocabulary

angle: the amount of turn between two lines meeting at a common point.

degrees: a unit for measuring the size of an angle.

Let's investigate

John has drawn four different triangles and measured the angles in each triangle. Here are all of his measurements. Find four groups of three angles that go together to make the angles of triangles. (Do not use the same size angle for more than one triangle.)

90°	63°	30°	17°
107°	53°	43°	50°
60°	100°	40°	67°

The angles of a triangle add up to 180°.

1   Helen drew this triangle.

She tore off the corners of the triangle along the dotted lines and put all the corners together.

Describe the angle made by the three angles of the triangle put together.

2   Measure two of the angles in each triangle and then calculate the size of the third angle.

Write down all three angles of each triangle to the nearest 5°.

(a)

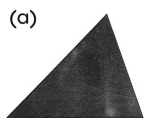

(b)

(c)

(d)

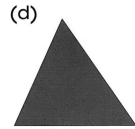

(e)

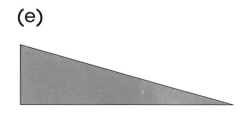

3   Tomas measures one of the angles of an
    equilateral triangle.

    It is 60°.

    What are the other two angles of the triangle?

    Explain how you know.

4   Professor Young has left instructions on which
    triangles need to go in to his *triangulator* machine.
    It just needs a few more pieces, all shaped as
    isosceles triangles. Unfortunately something has
    spilt on the instructions so that only one of the angle
    measurements for each shape is visible. Work out
    what the missing angles could be:

Machine Piece	Angle 1	Angle 2	Angle 3
(a)	80°		
(b)	45°		
(c)	54°		
(d)	12°		
(e)	37°		

Isosceles triangles have two
angles the same, and one
different.

The given angle could be the
same as one of the other angles
or the other two angles must be
the same as each other.

(f)   The Professor rings through the instructions for
      one more isosceles triangle piece, but it is not
      a good telephone line.

      There is only one solution to this isosceles triangle.

      What is it?

      Explain how you know there
      is not another solution.

      The last isoceles
      triangle piece has
      Angle 1 ☆☆degrees,
      Angle 2 ☆☆degrees, and
      Angle 3 will be 116 degrees.
      Must go. Bye!

Describing translations

Let's investigate

Nour makes this pattern by repeating the translation of a triangle.

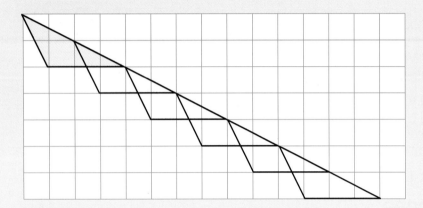

Describe to a partner how to make Nour's pattern.

Find, or draw, patterns of your own using translations.

Vocabulary

axis: is a reference line; graphs have a horizontal axis (x) and a vertical axis (y).

co-ordinates: show position on a grid; they are shown as pairs of numbers, for example $(-3, -1)$.

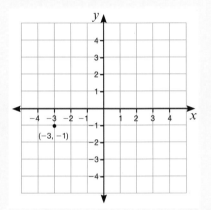

translation: moves or slides an item without rotating it.

1   Copy the diagram of a quadrilateral onto a square grid.

Translate the quadrilateral four squares to the right.

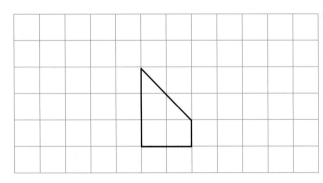

2   Which of these pieces fits the hole in the middle of the jigsaw?

3   Draw axes from −8 to +8 on squared paper. Draw a trapezium with co-ordinates (2, 1), (4, 1), (4, 5) and (2, 3). Label it X.

Translate X to a new position following these rules.
(a) to A by translating +3 in the *x*-direction
(b) to B by translating −6 in the *y*-direction
(c) to C by translating −6 in the *x*-direction and −4 in the *y*-direction
(d) to D by translating −7 in the *x*-direction and +3 in the *y*-direction

Write down the co-ordinates for shapes A, B, C and D.

4   Look at the triangles on the grid.

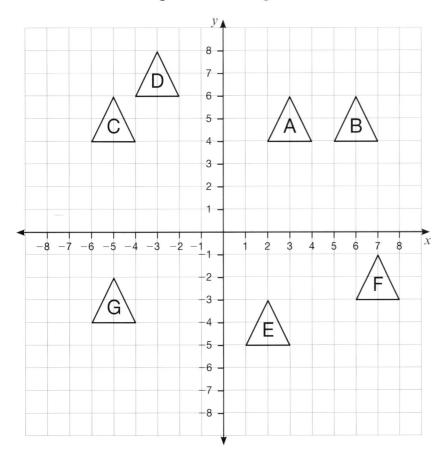

Write down the co-ordinates of the three vertices of:
(a) triangle A   **(b)** triangle C   **(c)** triangle G   **(d)** triangle F

5   Use the same grid. Describe the following translations:
(a) A to B   **(b)** B to C   **(c)** C to G   **(d)** A to E
(e) F to E   **(f)** G to E   **(g)** D to E   **(h)** F to G

Reflecting shapes

Let's investigate

This sheet of paper has been folded once.

The shape is cut out as shown.

Describe the final shape you would get if you opened it out.

How many lines of symmetry will it have?

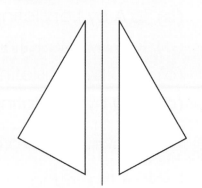

Vocabulary

reflection: a mirror view.

image: position of shape following a reflection.

1   Copy the diagram. Reflect the shape in the mirror line.

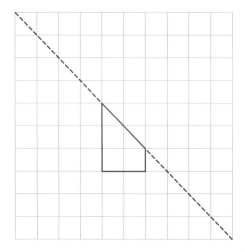

2   The diagram shows a shaded square on a grid.

   Draw a similar grid and shade in three more squares so the design is symmetrical about both mirror lines.

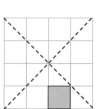

3   The line AB is a reflection of the
    line CD in a mirror line.

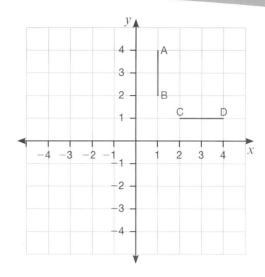

Draw the diagram and mark in the mirror line.

List all the points with whole number co-ordinates that lie on
the mirror line.

What do you notice about the co-ordinates of these points?

4   The diagram shows three squares
    on a co-ordinate grid.

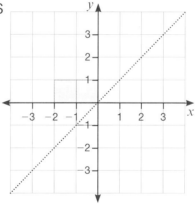

Decide where to place two more squares to make the pattern
symmetrical about the mirror line.

What are the co-ordinates of the vertices of the two squares?

5   (a) Draw a grid with x and y axes from -4 to $+4$.

    Join the point $(-4, 4)$ to the origin $(0,0)$.

    Reflect this line in the y-axis, then reflect the line and its
    image in the x-axis.

    What mathematical sign have you made?

    (b) Write instructions to make an addition sign using a line and reflecting
    it in different ways.

Rotation

Let's investigate

Look at the isosceles triangle drawn on a grid.

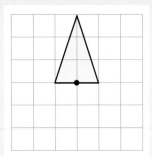

Rotate the triangle 90° clockwise about the •

Draw the image.

Continue rotating the triangle twice more.

What shape have you made?

Investigate rotating similar shapes you see during the day. Write a report on your findings.

You might find tracing paper helpful.

Vocabulary

rotation: turns an object about a point.

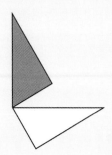

clockwise: the same direction as hands on a clock turn.

anti-clockwise: the opposite direction as hands on a clock turn.

1   The hour hand on an analogue clock points to 10.
    It turns through 90° clockwise.
    What number does it point to?

2   The diagram shows a trapezium on a square grid.
    Copy the shape on squared paper.
    Rotate the trapezium 90° clockwise about point A and draw the image.

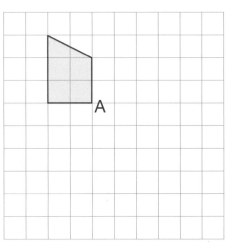

3   The diagram shows an octagon on a 12 by 12 square grid.
    Copy the shape onto squared paper.

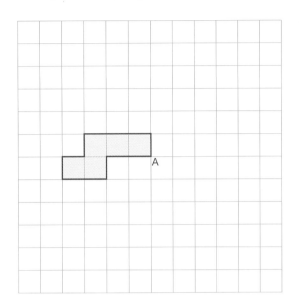

Rotate the octagon 90° clockwise about point A and draw the image.
Rotate the new image 90° clockwise about A again two more times,
each time drawing the image.

4   Look at the shaded shape on the grid.

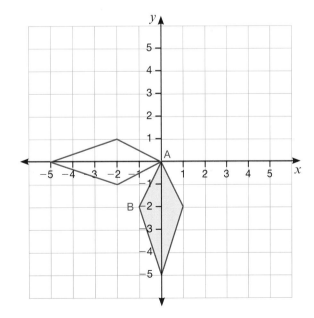

The shape is rotated 90° clockwise. Point A stays in the same place
but point B moves. What are the co-ordinates of the image of point B?

Number

The number system (1)

Let's investigate

Ali is thinking of a number.

When I round my number to the nearest 10 the answer is 1080. When I round my answer to the nearest 100 the answer is 1100.

What is the **smallest** number Ali could be thinking of?

What is the **largest** number Ali could be thinking of?

Look at question 1 to give you a clue.

1   A number rounded to the nearest 10 is 50. What could the number be?

2   [?] rounded to the nearest 10 is 700. What could the missing number be?

3   Write in figures a number that is bigger than one thousand but smaller than one thousand one hundred.

4   Find a whole number to make this statement true.

24 000 < [?] < 25 000

5   Copy the number line below and draw an arrow (↓) to show the position of 8500 on the number line.

6 Look at the number line and then complete the statements.

6000

(a) The number 6000 is half way between [ ] and 7200.

(b) The number 6000 is half way between 1500 and [ ].

7 Which number is closer to 10 000?

9960 or 10 060?

Explain how you know.

8 A holiday costs between $1600 and $2100.

Which of these prices could be the cost of the holiday?

$1569 $2090 $2130 $1999

The decimal system

Let's investigate

Maria is thinking of a decimal number less than 1.

> The hundreths digit is four more than the tenths digit. The sum of the tenths digit and the hundreths digit is 10.

What number is Maria thinking of?

1   Write these numbers in order of size, starting with the smallest.

   (a) 1.01   1.1   0.1   0.11   0.01

   (b) 0.19   0.9   0.91   0.09   0.11

2   Find four examples that make this general statement correct.

   If 0.24 < ? < 0.27 then any number between 0.24 and 0.27 can go in the box.

3   The students in a class had a sponsored swim. They collected $429.24.

   (a) How much is $429.24 to the nearest hundred dollars?

   (b) How much is $429.24 to the nearest ten dollars?

   (c) How much is $429.24 to the nearest dollar?

   (d) How much is $429.24 to the nearest tenth of a dollar?

4   (a) Find the number that is half way between 2.8 and 3.4.

   (b) Complete this statement. The number 6 is halfway between 2.8 and ? .

5   Write down the value of the digit 9 in each of these numbers.

   (a) 72.9   (b) 392.75   (c) 4.69

   (d) 13.09   (e) 19.11   (f) 9.06

6   Write these numbers in figures:

   (a) fifteen point one five.

   (b) one hundred and seven point zero seven.

7 Find the missing numbers.

(a) $7.2 \times 100 = $?   (b) $0.75 \times 100 = $?   (c) $4.28 \times 10 = $?

(d) $27.3 \div 100 = $?   (e) $151 \div 100 = $?   (f) $6.6 \div 10 = $?

8 Find the missing numbers.

(a) ? $\times 0.6 = 6$ (b) $103 \div$? $= 1.03$ (c) ? $\times 0.13 = 13$

(d) $7.6 \div$? $= 0.076$ (e) ? $\times 4.1 = 410$ (f) $0.09 \times$? $= 90$

9 What number is shown by the arrow on this number line?

10 Ten times a number is 3.5. What is the number?

11 Use each of the digits 1, 2, 4 and 9 to make the number that is closest to 20.

12 Find a number where all the digits are odd and the sum of the digits is 7.

?	?	.	?

Can you find more than one answer?

13 Here are eight numbers:

1.25   0.05   0.48   0.218   0.4   0.004   0.875   0.375

Use the clues to identify one of these numbers:

- the number is less than 1
- the number is greater than 0.3
- the tenths digit is even
- the hundredths digit is even
- one hundred times the number gives a whole number answer
- the number multiplied by 10 gives an answer greater than 0.4.

14 A number is 11.7 when rounded to the nearest tenth.

(a) What are all the possible numbers with two decimal places that it could be?

(b) What is the number rounded to the nearest whole number?

Operations with decimals

Let's investigate

In a magic square, the numbers add up to the same number vertically, horizontally or diagonally.

This magic square must add up to 1.5.

Complete the square.

		0.6
	0.5	
0.4		

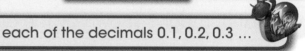

Use each of the decimals 0.1, 0.2, 0.3 ...

1   Work out the answers to these calculations.
   (a) 4.5 + 2.68   **(b)** 7.1 + 9.45   **(c)** 3.8 + 7.09
   (d) 5.1 + 3.92   **(e)** 4.6 + 4.76   **(f)** 4.3 + 5.99
   Which of the answers are less than 10?

2   Five of the answers to the following calculations are in this grid. Work out the answers to these calculations. Which answer is missing?

2.58	1.34	7.20
2.15	5.13	4.76

   (a) 9.23 − 4.1   **(b)** 8.16 − 3.4   **(c)** 4.28 − 1.7
   (d) 9.4 − 2.38   **(e)** 7.6 − 5.45   **(f)** 3.2 − 1.86
   Which number in the grid is not an answer to any of the calculations?

3   **(a)** What do you need to add to 4.79 to make 10?
   (b) What do you need to take away from 10 to make 5.36?

4   Find the missing numbers.
   (a) 4.8 + **?** = 10   **(b)** **?** + 3.6 = 10   **(c)** 3.7 + 6.3 = **?**
   (d) 10 − 3.7 = **?**   **(e)** 10 − **?** = 8.1   **(f)** **?** − 4.6 = 5.4

5   Find the missing digits.

```
    8 · ? 7                 3 · ? 6
  −   ? · 6 ?             +   ? · 8 ?
    _____             _____
    3 · 6 9                 1 · 3 5
```

6 (a) What is double 15.5?

(b) What is half of 14.5?

7 Which two of the following numbers add to make 1?

0.1   0.3   0.03   0.7   0.07   0.2

8 Decimal pyramids are built like this:

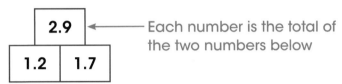

Each number is the total of the two numbers below

Build these pyramids.

(a)

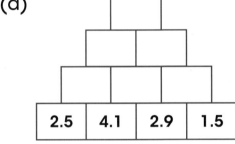

| 2.5 | 4.1 | 2.9 | 1.5 |

(b)

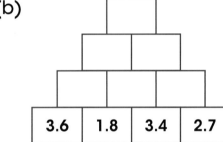

| 3.6 | 1.8 | 3.4 | 2.7 |

(c)

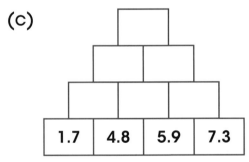

| 1.7 | 4.8 | 5.9 | 7.3 |

(d)

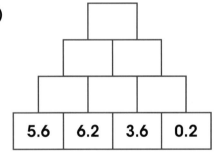

| 5.6 | 6.2 | 3.6 | 0.2 |

9 Write down five pairs of one-place decimals that add up to 10.
- What do the units digits of each pair add up to?
- What do the tenths digits of each pair add up to?

10 Arrange the numbers 0.1, 0.2, 0.3, 0.4, 0.5 and 0.6 so that the sum of the numbers on the vertical line is the same as the sum of the numbers in the horizontal line.

Decimals in context

Let's investigate

Cheng buys five presents. She spends a total of $20.

- The total cost of A and B is $7.00.
- The total cost of B and C is $6.00.
- The total cost of C and D is $7.00.
- The total cost of D and E is $9.00.

What is the cost of each present?

Use trial and improvement.
Remember to be systematic.

1 A swimming pool is 50 metres long and 25 metres wide. How many lengths of the pool will a competitor in a 1500 metre race have to swim?

2 Hamda buys a 2 kilogram bag of tomatoes. She uses 400 grams of tomatoes to make soup. How many grams of tomatoes has she left?

3 Roz has a 2 metre length of ribbon. She cuts off a piece of ribbon 65 centimetres long. How much ribbon is left?

4 A triangle has sides of length 5 cm, 12 cm and 13 cm. What is the perimeter of the triangle?

5 A jug holds 1 litre of water.
   Fatima pours out 90 millilitres of water.
   How many millilitres of water is left in the jug?

6 A bucket holds 2.75 litres of water.
   How many millilitres is this?

7   What is 200 g + 1.9 kg
    Give your answer in grams.

8   Ali goes cycling. He cycles 65 km on the first day and 43 km on the
    second day. How far does he cycle altogether?

9   Ahmed goes on a 12 kilometre hike. How many metres does he travel?

10 Bruno is measuring water for an experiment. He fills a 2 litre container
    and a half litre container. How much water does Bruno use altogether?
    Give your answer in millilitres.

11 Chimgee buys a bracelet for $3.25. She gives the cashier $5.00.
    How much change does she get?

12 Vincent pays $4.15 for sandwiches and $0.85 for a piece of fruit.
    What is the total cost of the sandwiches and fruit?

13 A bargain bookshop is offering
    $2.50 discount off these books.
    What is the sale price of each book?

    $6.25 $9.10 $13.35

14 Find the total cost of three items costing $9.45, $15.05 and $3.64.

15 A T-shirt costs $7.75 in a half price sale. What was the full price?

16 A puzzle costs $0.65. How many puzzles can Madi buy for $2
    How much change does she get?

17 Two friends go to a restaurant for a meal.
    The meals cost $19.45 and $18.86.
    Khalid has $40 to pay for the two meals.
    How much change does he get?

18 A shop sells three types of sweatshirt.
    They are priced at $24.69, $12.99 and $15.85
    What is the difference in price between the most expensive
    and the least expensive?

Positive and negative numbers

Vocabulary

Let's investigate

The difference between two numbers is 3.

One number is −2.

What could the other number be?

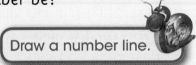
Draw a number line.

positive: a positive number is greater than zero.

negative: a negative number is less than zero.

We use a − sign to show a negative number.

zero: is another name for 'nothing' or 'nought'.

On a number line it is the point where numbers change from positive to negative.

1   Which numbers are marked with crosses on the number lines?

   (a)

   (b)

2   The table shows the minimum temperature on four days.

Day	Temperature °C
Monday	−2
Tuesday	1
Wednesday	3
Thursday	−4

Write the temperatures in order, starting with the coldest temperature.

3   Write each set of temperatures in order, starting with the coldest temperature.

   (a) −4 °C   1 °C   −8 °C   −2 °C   3 °C

   (b) −2 °C   4 °C   −7 °C   −13 °C   13 °C

   (c) 6 °C   −6 °C   0 °C   −7 °C   −4 °C

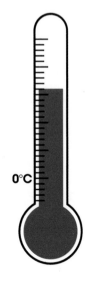

4 The temperature at 8 pm is −2 °C. By midnight it is 6° colder.
What is the temperature at midnight?

5 The temperature at 8 am is −1 °C. By midday it is 4° warmer.
What is the temperature at midday?

6 The maximum temperature in Mongolia during October is 15 °C.
The temperature decreases by 12° each month from October to February
What is the maximum temperature in January?

7 Here is part of a number line.
What are the missing numbers?

8 What is the difference between these pairs of numbers.
(a) 6 and −2   (b) −3 and −5   (c) −4 and −8
(d) −5 and 3   (e) −6 and −1   (f) 0 and −2

9 Here is part of a number line.

The difference between A and B is 20. What is the value of A?

10 Use each of the numbers −2, −3, −4 and −5 once to make the
inequalities correct.

? < ?

? > ?

11 Which two of the following numbers have a difference of 2?

1.5   1   0.5   −0.5   −1

Multiples and factors

Let's investigate

A light flashes every four minutes and a bell rings every five minutes.

If the light flashes as the bell rings at the same time, how long will it be until this happens again?

Think about the multiples of 4 and 5.

Vocabulary

common multiple: a multiple that is shared by two or more numbers. For example,

- 12 is a common multiple of 2 and 3 because 12 is a multiple of both 2 and 3.

- 12 is a common multiple of 6 and 4 because 12 is a multiple of both 6 and 4.

- 12 is a common multiple of 2, 3, 4 and 6.

1 Find two factors of 24 that total 11.

2 Choose three of these numbers to make a correct number sentence.

21 22 23 24 25 26 27 28 29

$\boxed{?}$ + $\boxed{?}$ + $\boxed{?}$ = a multiple of 10

3 Vijay is thinking of a number.

It is under 20.
It is a multiple of 3.
It is a multiple of 5.

What number is Vijay thinking

4   Copy the Venn diagram. Write the numbers 3, 4, 5, 6 and 7 in the correct place in your Venn diagram.

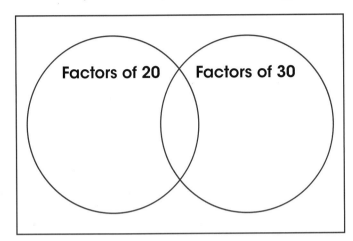

5   What is the smallest number that is a multiple of 8 and 12?
    How do you know?

6   Explain why a number ending in 1 cannot be a multiple of 2.

7   Copy and complete this Venn diagram using all the numbers from 1 to 15.

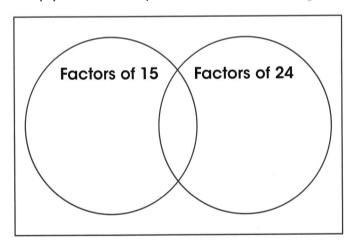

8   Copy the Carroll diagram. Put the numbers 10, 11, 12, 13, 14, 15, 16, 17, 18, 19 and 20 in the correct position on the Carroll diagram.

	multiple of 2	not multiples of 2
multiples of 4		
not multiples of 4		

Why will one of the cells on the diagram never have any numbers in it?

1   Here are some examples of calculation strategies.
Some are correct but some are not.

Say whether each example is correct or not.
If it is incorrect, give a correct strategy.

> Remember: always ask yourself, 'Can I do the calculation mentally?' before writing anything down.

	Calculation	Strategy
(a)	3456 − 1997	3456 − 2000 + 3
(b)	427 + 199	427 + 200 + 1
(c)	4865 + 299	4865 + 300 − 1
(d)	4824 − 2997	4824 − 3000 − 3
(e)	9843 − 7997	9843 − 8000 + 3

2   Copy and complete the spider diagrams to show other facts that
can be derived from the fact in the centre of the diagram.

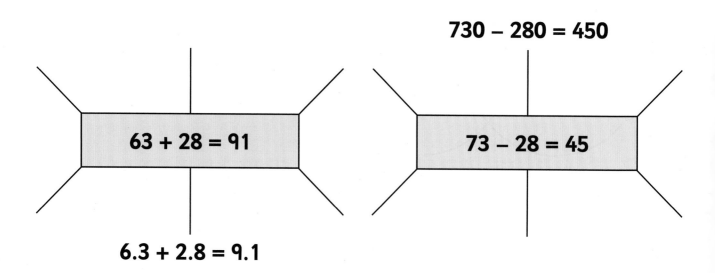

730 − 280 = 450

63 + 28 = 91

73 − 28 = 45

6.3 + 2.8 = 9.1

3 Answer these questions using a mental strategy:

(a) What number is one hundred and ninety nine more than five hundred and twenty seven?

(b) What is the difference between one thousand, nine hundred and ninety four, and four thousand and three?

(c) Find the total of nine hundred and ninety seven and four hundred and thirteen.

Mental strategies for multiplication

There are many ways in which you can use table facts to help you multiply larger numbers. Use the example methods to answer the questions.

A 100 square has been supplied to help you if you need it.

Vocabulary

near multiple of 10: a number either side of a multiple of 10. For example, 20 is a multiple of 10 so 19 and 21 are near multiples of 10.

×	1	2	3	4	5	6	7	8	9	10
1	1	2	3	4	5	6	7	8	9	10
2	2	4	6	8	10	12	14	16	18	20
3	3	6	9	12	15	18	21	24	27	30
4	4	8	12	16	20	24	28	32	36	40
5	5	10	15	20	25	30	35	40	45	50
6	6	12	18	24	30	36	42	48	54	60
7	7	14	21	28	35	42	49	56	63	70
8	8	16	24	32	40	48	56	64	72	80
9	9	18	27	36	45	54	63	72	81	90
10	10	20	30	40	50	60	70	80	90	100

1   Here is a method for calculating 15×7:

$$10 \times 7 = 70$$
$$5 \times 7 = 35$$
$$15 \times 7 = 105$$

Use this method to work out:

(a) 18×7 (b) 19×5 (c) 13×7 (d) 17×9

(e) 17×8 (f) 18×9 (g) 16×8 (h) 15×5

2   Here is method for calculating 39×5:

$$40 \times 5 = 200$$
$$1 \times 5 = 5 \quad -$$
$$\overline{39 \times 5 = 195}$$

Use this method to work out:

(a) 49×7 (b) 49×6 (c) 59×8 (d) 39×4

(e) 59×7 (f) 79×4 (g) 89×6 (h) 99×8

3   Here is a method for calculating 41×6:

$$40 \times 6 = 240$$
$$1 \times 6 = 6 \quad -$$
$$\overline{41 \times 6 = 246}$$

Use this method to work out:

(a) 31×3 (b) 61×9 (c) 91×7 (d) 51×8

(e) 81×9 (f) 41×7 (g) 21×7 (h) 71×8

4   You know that $42 \times 8 = 336$ so, $21 \times 16 = 336$ (double one number and halve the other)

Use this method to work out:

(a) If $21 \times 84 = 1764$, what is 42×42?

(b) If $14 \times 37 = 518$, what is 28×18.5?

Use a written strategy or a calulator to check that the mental strategy works for each of these examples.

Divisibility rules

Let's investigate

Find the smallest number
that is divisible by 2, 3, 4 and 5.

> Make lists of the multiples or shade them in on a hundred square.

Vocabulary

divisible: can be divided without a remainder. For example, 14 is divisible by 2.

Number	Test of divisibility
2	The units digit is divisible by 2
4	The number made by the last two digits is divisible by 4
5	The units digit is 5 or 0
10	The units digit is 0
25	The last two digits are 00, 25, 50 or 75
100	The last two digits are 00

1   Which of these numbers will divide exactly by 2?
    Explain how you know.

    34   37   29   48   260   216   2370

2   Which of these numbers will divide exactly by 4?
    Explain how you know.

    74   37   92   84   260   216   2372

3   Complete this three-digit number so that it is divisible by 4.

    | 2 | ? | ? | = a number divisible by 4.

4   Use the digits 3, 4, 5 and 6 to complete the number sentence.
    The sum of the two numbers is divisible by 5.

    | ? | ? | + | ? | ? | = a number divisible by 5

5   Decide which of these statements are true and which are false.
    Give a reason for each decision.

    Example:

    | **142 is divisible by 4** | False, because 42 is not a multiple of 4.

    (a) 324 is divisible by 4
    (b) 53 is not divisible by 2
    (c) 1000 is not divisible by 10
    (d) 41 is divisible by 5
    (e) 775 is divisible by 25
    (f) 34.0 is divisible by 10
    (g) 580 is not divisible by 25
    (h) 2005 is divisible by 100

Multiplication

Let's investigate

Two consecutive numbers multiply together to make 650.

What are the two numbers?

| $20 \times 20 = 400$ |
| $30 \times 30 = 900$ |

Make up some more puzzles like this and swap them with a partner.

Vocabulary

consecutive: next to each other. For example, 7 and 8 are consecutive whole numbers.

1 Work out these multiplications using the grid method.

   (a) 164×5

$\times$	100	60	4
5			

   (b) 327×8

$\times$	300	20	7
8			

2 (a) Estimate the answer to 86×7

   (b) Calculate 86×7

3 Work out the following calculations:

   (a)
   ```
     298
   ×   4
   ─────
   ```
   (b)
   ```
     418
   ×   3
   ─────
   ```
   (c)
   ```
     596
   ×   2
   ─────
   ```
   (d)
   ```
     209
   ×   6
   ─────
   ```

   What do you notice about the answers to (a) and (c) and the answers to (b) and (d)?

   Explain why this happened.

4 Calculate:

   (a) 32×83 (b) 57×61 (c) 48×56

   (d) 24×92 (e) 47×34 (f) 36×54

5 Use these digits 0, 1, 3 and 5 to complete this calculation.
   You must use each digit only once.

   $\boxed{?}\,\boxed{?} \times \boxed{?}\,\boxed{?} = 450$

6 (a) Find the product of 136 and 9.
   (b) Multiply 35 by 16.
   (c) Find the product of 98 and 7.

7 Calculate $19 \times 5 \times 6$

8 Write in the missing digits to make this calculation correct.

$$
\begin{array}{r}
\boxed{?}\;7\;\boxed{?} \\
\times \qquad 6 \\
\hline
1\;0\;3\;2 \\
\hline
\end{array}
$$

9 Use the digits 3, 4, 5 and 6 to complete this calculation:

   $\boxed{?}\,\boxed{?} \times \boxed{?}\,\boxed{?}$

   (a) to make the largest possible answer
   (b) to make the smallest possible answer.

10 In this multiplication each shape stands for a different digit.
   Work out what each shape stands for?

$$
\begin{array}{r}
\pentagon\;\square \\
\times \qquad 5\;\square \\
\hline
\square\;1\;\triangle\;\triangle \\
8\;\pentagon \\
\hline
\square\;1\;8\;\pentagon \\
\hline
\end{array}
$$

11 Find different ways of completing this calculation:

   $\boxed{?}\,\boxed{?} \times \boxed{?} = 256$

12 (a) Find two consecutive numbers with a product of 182.
   (b) Find two consecutive numbers with a product of 870.

13 Use each of the digits 1 to 6 to make a correct calculation:

   $\boxed{?}\,\boxed{?} \times \boxed{?} = \boxed{?}\,\boxed{?}\,\boxed{?}$

Division (2)

Let's investigate

- Choose a three-digit number with all the digits the same.
- Add the digits.
- Divide your original number by your addition answer.
- Record the result.

Repeat with different starting numbers. What do you notice?

> Example:
> 666
> $6 + 6 + 6 = 18$
> $666 \div 18 = 37$

1 Estimate first and then work out these calculations:

    (a) $104 \div 4$ **(b)** $168 \div 7$ **(c)** $342 \div 6$

    (d) $423 \div 9$ **(e)** $472 \div 8$ **(f)** $305 \div 5$

2 Work out these division calculations. They all have a remainder.

    (a) $351 \div 6$ **(b)** $509 \div 9$ **(c)** $398 \div 8$

    (d) $375 \div 4$ **(e)** $436 \div 7$ **(f)** $296 \div 3$

3 What is the missing digit?

    | ? | 7 | $\times\ 9 = 333$

4 Give the answers to these calculations including a remainder.

    (a) $254 \div 9$ **(b)** $345 \div 6$ **(c)** $396 \div 7$

5 Give the answers to these calculations including a remainder.

    (a) $964 \div 5$ **(b)** $305 \div 2$ **(c)** $231 \div 4$

6 Find the missing number?

    | ? | $\div\ 5 = 22$

7 How many groups of eight can be made from 100?

8 **(a)** Divide 112 by 7.   **(b)** Divide 7 into 224.   **(c)** Share 207 between 9.

Special numbers

Let's investigate

Place the numbers 1, 2, 3, 4, 5, 6, 7, 8 and 9 in the squares so the sum of the three numbers in each row and column is a prime number.

Make a list of the prime numbers to 20.

1   Identify the following numbers.

(a) The number is even.
It is a multiple of 4.
It is a factor of 24.
It is between 10 and 20.

(b) The number is less than 80.
It is a multiple of 5.
The sum of the digits is 9.
It is odd.

(c) The number is prime.
It is less than 50.
It has two digits which are both the same.

(d) The number has 9 factors.
It is between 10 and 99.
The sum of the digits is 9.
It is even.
It is a square number.

2   Explain whether these statements are true or false. Explain your answer.

(a) Every multiple of 5 ends in 5.

(b) If you double an odd number the answer is always even.

(c) When you halve an even number the answer is always odd.

(d) All prime numbers are odd.

(e) A multiple of 4 can never end in 3.

(f) All numbers that end in 4 are multiples of 4.

(g) When you halve a number ending in 8 the answer will always end in 4.

Measure

Mass and capacity

Let's investigate

One litre of petrol weighs approximately 700 g.

The mass of my car was 1228 kg when I started my journey. At the end of the journey it was 1214.7 kg.

If I did not change the mass of the car in any way, except using the petrol, how many litres of petrol had I used?

Vocabulary

capacity: the amount a container can hold.

liquid volume: the space taken up by a liquid.

litre: a unit of capacity or liquid volume.

millilitre: a unit of capacity or liquid volume, one thousandth of a litre.

mass: quantity of matter in an object.

gram: a unit of mass.

kilogram: a unit of mass, one thousand grams.

Look at the scales on the measuring equipment on the page opposite. Match each ingredient to the equipment showing the same amount. Write the number of the ingredient and the letter of the equipment.

1

1.3 kg

2

850 ml

3

950 g

4

275 g

5

0.33 g

6

280 ml

7

2.4 kg

8

1.8 l

FIZZ

9

68 g

10

1.72 kg

11

25 ml

12

4.6 l

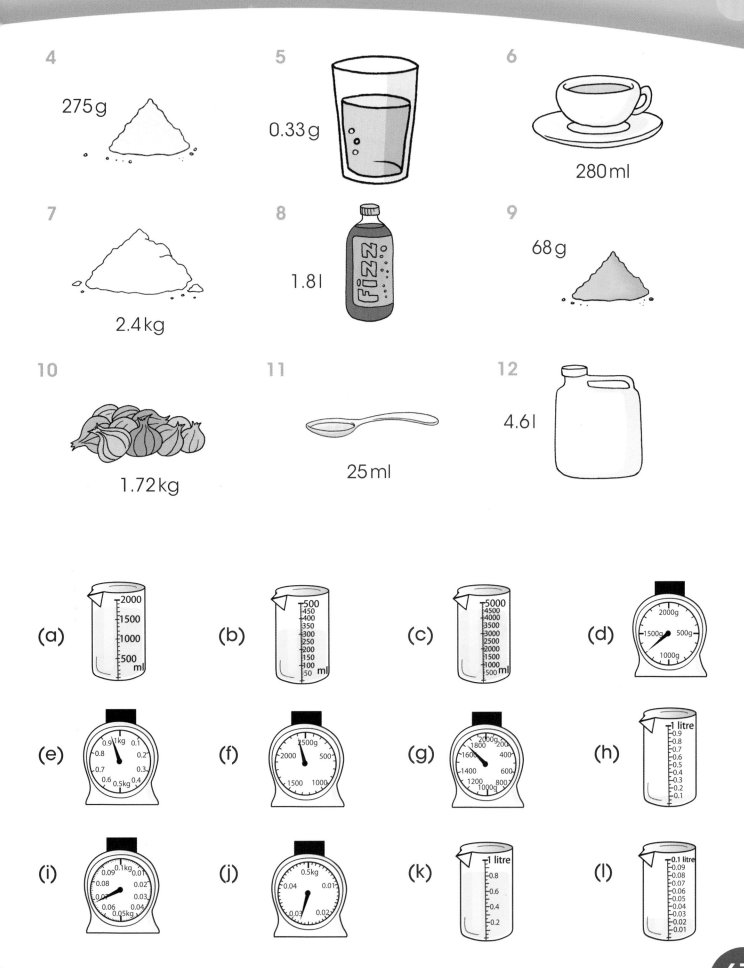

(a) 2000 / 1500 / 1000 / 500 ml

(b) 500 / 450 / 400 / 350 / 300 / 250 / 200 / 150 / 100 / 50 ml

(c) 5000 / 4500 / 4000 / 3500 / 3000 / 2500 / 2000 / 1500 / 1000 / 500 ml

(d) 2000g / 1500g / 500g / 1000g

(e) 1kg / 0.9 / 0.8 / 0.7 / 0.6 / 0.5kg / 0.4 / 0.3 / 0.2 / 0.1

(f) 2500g / 2000 / 500 / 1500 / 1000

(g) 2000g / 1800 / 200 / 1600 / 400 / 1400 / 600 / 1200 / 800 / 1000g

(h) 1 litre / 0.9 / 0.8 / 0.7 / 0.6 / 0.5 / 0.4 / 0.3 / 0.2 / 0.1

(i) 0.1kg / 0.09 / 0.01 / 0.08 / 0.02 / 0.07 / 0.03 / 0.06 / 0.04 / 0.05kg

(j) 0.5kg / 0.04 / 0.01 / 0.03 / 0.02

(k) 1 litre / 0.8 / 0.6 / 0.4 / 0.2

(l) 0.1 litre / 0.09 / 0.08 / 0.07 / 0.06 / 0.05 / 0.04 / 0.03 / 0.02 / 0.01

13 This is a recipe for vegetable soup.

Country Vegetable Soup
Recipe for 1 person

Ingredients

70 g carrots

25 g onion

20 g mushrooms

90 g leek

225 g potato

8 g garlic

330 ml water

15 ml vegetable oil

Calculate the amounts of each ingredient needed for the recipe if it was for 20 people. Convert grams to kilograms and millilitres to litres.

14 This is a recipe for pancakes.

Pancake Recipe
Makes 15 pancakes

Ingredients

2 cups of flour

2 eggs

2½ cups of milk

Calculate the amounts of each ingredient needed if it was for 30 people.
Give your answer in metric units.

grams	cups	millilitres
750 —	5 —	— 1200
	4 —	— 1000
500 —	3 —	— 800
		— 600
250 —	2 —	— 400
	1 —	— 200
0 —	0 —	— 0

Use the conversion scale to find approximate metric measures.
1 cup of flour = approx. 150 g
1 cup of milk = approx. 240 ml

Calculating Time

Let's investigate

Rani needs to get to a dance lesson today by 20:25. If the clock shows the time now, how long does she have until her lesson?

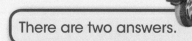
There are two answers.

1   Write whether each of these statements is true or false.

   (a) One week is more than 100 hours.

   (b) There are more weeks in a year than days in two months.

   (c) There are more than 85 000 seconds in one day.

   (d) One week is less than 10 000 minutes.

   (e) There are more months with 30 days than 31 days.

   (f) There are more than 750 hours in one month.

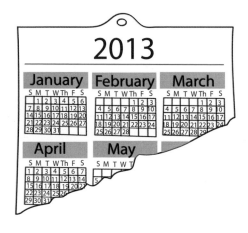  

2 Ten athletes competed in a marathon run.

These are their times:

Florence	141 minutes and 32 seconds
Emmanuel	2 hours, 8 minutes and 39 seconds
Mai	174 minutes and 18 seconds
Yared	2 hours and 1302 seconds
Susan	158 minutes and 55 seconds
Paul	2 hours and 554 seconds
Emily	3 hours, 2 minutes and 49 seconds
Gianmarco	159 minutes and 5 seconds
Maria	3 hours and 183 seconds
Kazuyoshi	8127 seconds

Make a table showing the results in order of the time taken to run the marathon, fastest to slowest.

3 Use your table to find out what was the time difference between:

(a) Florence and Yared

(b) Emmanuel and Paul

(c) Kazuyoshi and Mai

(d) Susan and Maria

(e) Emmanuel and Maria.

> Convert all the times into the same unit.
> Remember there are 60 minutes in an hour, and 60 seconds in a minute.

Time Zones (1)

Let's investigate

The time difference between where Marco and Cody live is 3 hours, Marco's time is ahead of Cody's. They have a telephone conversation for 1 hour and 18 minutes. Cody puts the phone down at 20:44.
What was the time for Marco when he rang?

This map shows *approximately* the time zones around the world. It shows how far ahead or behind the time is in hours from the Universal Time at '0'.

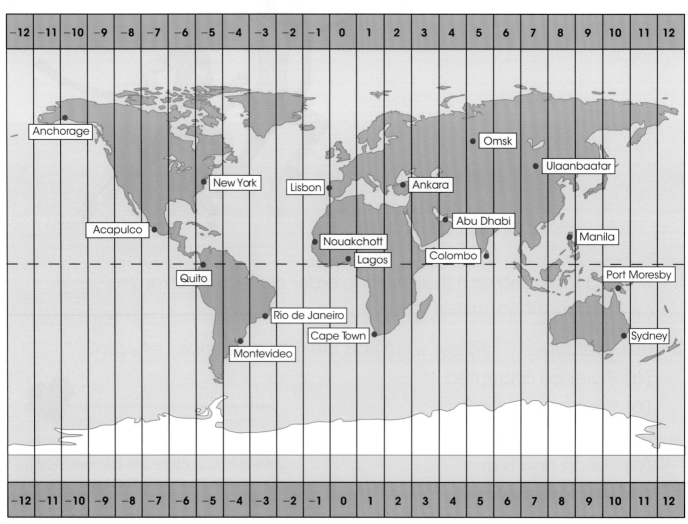

1 What is the approximate time difference in hours between:

(a) Quito and Lisbon?

(b) Anchorage and Colombo?

(c) Cape Town and Ulannbaatar?

(d) Nouakchott and Sydney?

2 Use the map to estimate:

(a) If it was 09:21 in Lagos, what would be the time in Omsk?

(b) If it was 01:44 in Acapulco, what would be the time in Port Moresby?

(c) If it was 18:03 in Rio de Janeiro, what would be the time in Ankara?

(d) If it was 20:18 in Manila, what would be the time in Colombo?

3 If it was midday in Colombo, which cities on the map would have
a different date to the date in Colombo?

Area and perimeter (2)

Let's investigate

this red and yellow tile is 36 cm². What is
the area of the red part of the tile?

You could visualise cutting the red parts
off the tile and placing them on the yellow
square to compare the red and yellow areas.

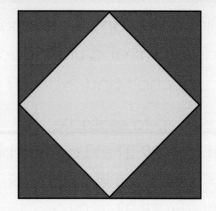

1   At a community picnic each family needs to lay down
    picnic blankets big enough for all of their family to sit on.

    (a) The Veselova family needs 19 000 cm².

    (b) The Whitmore family needs 14 800 cm².

    (c) The Shah family needs 15 900 cm².

    (d) The Juwe family needs 15 300 cm².

    (e) The Tharmarajah family needs 13 600 cm².

    You could work out the area
    of each blanket first and then
    add together combinations of
    two blankets to make the totals
    each family needs.

    Each family will use two picnic blankets. Which blankets should
    they put together to make the correct area? Only one family
    can use each blanket.

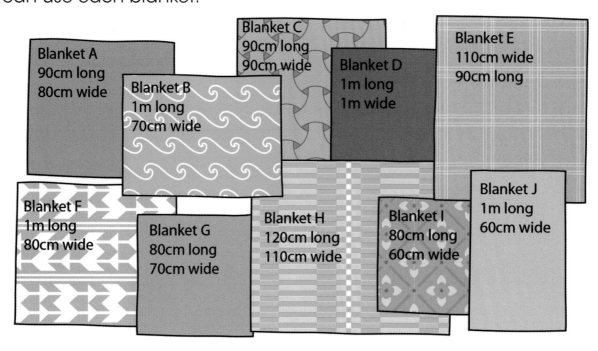

2 The costs of carpets in a local shop are shown in the picture.

(a) The first customer wants 30 m² of the blue carpet. How much would that cost?

(b) The second customer wants a green carpet to fit a rectangular room measuring 7 m long and 4 m wide. How much will it cost?

(c) The third customer wants a striped carpet for a square room measuring 5 m long and a pink carpet measuring 4 m long and 3 m wide. How much will that cost in total?

(d) The fourth customer wants a red carpet to fit this room. How much will it cost?

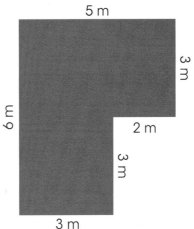

(e) The fifth customer wants carpet for a whole floor of their house. This is a plan of the house with the colours required for each room. What will be the total cost?

(f) What is the perimeter of the room with the red carpet?

(g) What is the perimeter of the room with the green carpet?

(h) What is the perimeter of the room with the purple carpet?

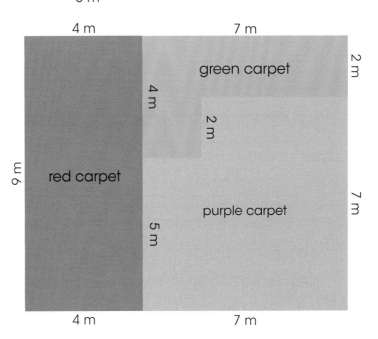

Handling data

Graphs and tables

Let's investigate

This graph shows how much water had dripped from a leaky tap in five minutes. Use the graph to work out how much water would have dripped from the tap in an hour.

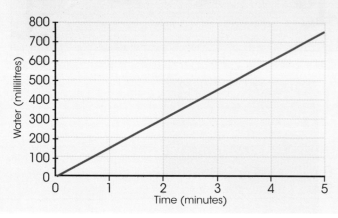

1   Copy and complete the currency conversion table.

Japanese Yen (¥)	Euro (€)	US Dollars ($)
130	1	130
	2	
	5	
	10	
	20	
	50	
	100	

2   (a) How many Japanese Yen are equivalent to €20?

(b) How many US Dollars are equivalent to ¥1300?

(c) How many Euros are equivalent to $6.50?

(d) How many Japanese Yen are equivalent to €6?

(e) How many US Dollars are equivalent to ¥3900?

(f) How many Euros are equivalent to $71.50?

3 Draw a line graph. Choose between:

- a line graph converting Japanese Yen to Euros,
- a line graph converting Japanese Yen to US Dollars, or
- a line graph converting Euros to US Dollars
- two currencies of your choice (you will need to look this up on the Internet!)

> Remember to choose the scale of the graph carefully. Work out the lowest and greatest values first.

4 This line graph shows the distance travelled when a vehicle is travelling at 30 kilometres per hour, compared to 40 kilometres per hour.

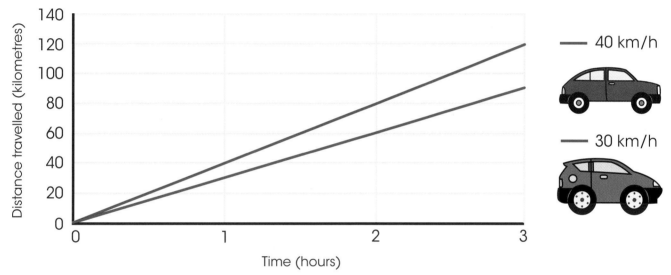

Use calculations **or** the line graph to solve these questions and then check your answers with the other method.

(a) How far will a car have travelled in 2 hours if it is travelling at 40 km/h?

(b) How far will a car have travelled in $2\frac{1}{2}$ hours if it is travelling at 30 km/h?

(c) How much further has a car travelled after $1\frac{1}{2}$ hours if it is travelling at 40 km/h rather than 30 km/h?

(d) How many kilometres will a car have travelled after 4 hours if it is travelling a 30mph?

(e) How many kilometres will a car have travelled after 10 hours if it is travelling 40 km/h?

(f) For this example, which method is better? Using calculations or reading from the graph?

Pie charts

pie chart: a graph using a divided circle where each section represents part of the total.

Let's investigate

George's friends voted on what they wanted to do during their holiday. Complete the key from the clues.

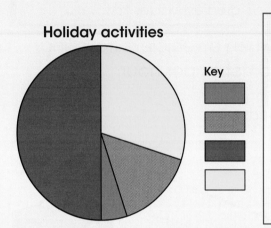

Holiday activities

Key

Clues

• Volleyball was more popular than horse riding

• Swimming had over 40% of the votes.

• Less than 10% of the friends voted for trampolining.

1   A pet shop sells a range of fish. This pie chart shows the fish that were sold in one week.

(a) What is the most common type of goldfish?

(b) If a total of 50 goldfish were sold in that week, estimate the number of each type of goldfish sold.

• Common Goldfish.

• Fantail Goldfish.

• Oranda Goldfish.

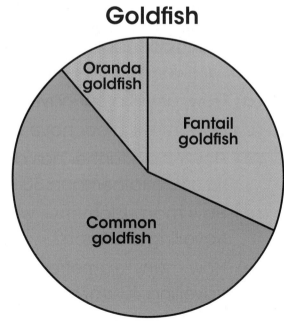

Goldfish

Oranda goldfish

Fantail goldfish

Common goldfish

2   The pet shop also sells tropical fish. This is a pie chart of the
    tropical fish sold that week.

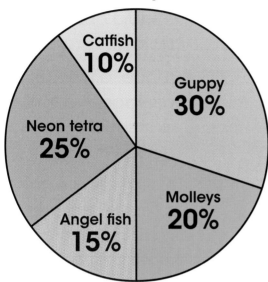

200 tropical fish were sold.

Draw a bar graph that represents the data from this pie chart.

Average and range

Let's investigate

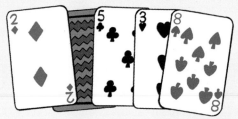

The mean average of the numbers on these cards is 5.

What number is on the fifth card?

1   Kali, Summer, Benji and Kyle and learning to skip.

   While they were practising they recorded how many skips they did in a row.

   Here are their attempts:

Bus	1st try	2nd try	3rd try	4th try	5th try	6th try	7th try
Kali	6	5	6	6	8	11	7
Summer	3	0	3	8	0	7	0
Benji	0	0	1	0	4	0	2
Kyle	4	7	7	6	2	5	4

(a) Copy and complete this table:

	Range	Mode	Median	Mean
Kali				
Summer				
Benji				
Kyle				

(b) Who do you think has been most successful at skipping?

Explain your answer using the information in your table.

average: a measure used to find the middle of a set of data.

mode: a type of average, the value in a set of data that occurs the most.

mean: a type of average, calculated by finding the total of all the values in the set of data and dividing by the number of values.

median: a type of average, the middle value in a set of values ordered from least to greatest.

range: from the lowest to the highest value.

2 Gabriella and Demi have recorded the temperature in the shade at midday on everyday of their six week school holiday.

	Sunday	Monday	Tuesday	Wednesday	Thursday	Friday	Saturday
Week 1	25 °C	20 °C	20 °C	19 °C	20 °C	24 °C	26 °C
Week 2	25 °C	25 °C	28 °C	27 °C	28 °C	31 °C	25 °C
Week 3	28 °C	27 °C	27 °C	27 °C	24 °C	22 °C	20 °C
Week 4	15 °C	19 °C	23 °C	19 °C	16 °C	15 °C	19 °C
Week 5	18 °C	19 °C	20 °C	23 °C	25 °C	28 °C	28 °C
Week 6	32 °C	32 °C	32 °C	27 °C	29 °C	28 °C	30 °C

(a) Design a table to record the three types of average and the range for each week of the holiday. Complete your table with the averages and range.

(b) Which week had the greatest range of temperatures?

(c) Use the information in your table to argue which was the warmest week of the holiday.

(d) Gabriella and Demi were taking part in a conservation project on every Tuesday of the holiday. What was the range of temperatures on Tuesdays?

What was the average (mode, median and mean) temperature on Tuesdays?

3 Use some of these cards to make sets of data to match these averages.

(a) mean 16, mode 16, median 16

(b) mean 17, mode 18, median 17.5

(c) mean 16, mode 15, median 15

Using statistics

Let's investigate

The council are planning transport for learners to and from school. This is what they found out about how 9 year old and 13 year old learners get to school.

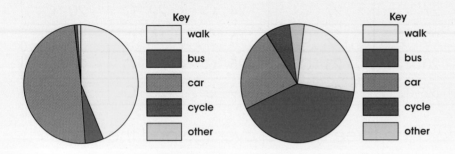

Describe the difference between how 9 year olds and 13 year olds go to school. What could be the explanations for these differences?

1   The four countries of Fratania, Spanila, Brimland and Gretilli celebrate a dry weather festival during the months of January to May. They are each trying to encourage tourists to visit their own countries. Here are graphs of each country's rainfall last year for the five months of the festival.

> **Vocabulary**
>
> statistics: the collection, organization, presentation, interpretation and analysis of data.

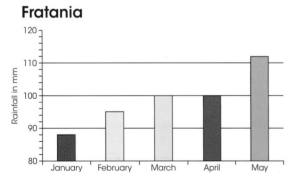

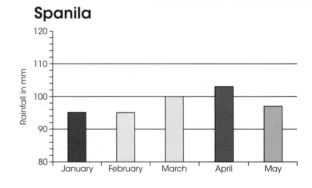

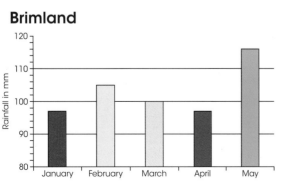

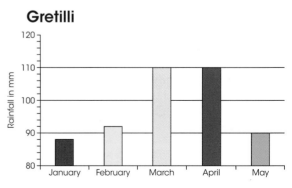

2 Which average (mode, median, or mean) would be best for each country to advertise the lowest possible average rainfall for the season?

3 With a group of learners, chose something that you think should change in your school or local area.

It could be to do with:

- places to play
- the attractiveness of the environment
- safety
- sports facilities
- another aspect of your school or local area that could be changed for the better.

As a group, collect data to show what the current situation is, such as:

- survey of other learners' opinions or experiences
- survey of how many/much of something there is, e.g. litter, traffic.

Organise the data in a table. If appropriate for your project, calculate statistics, such as average or range.

Chose a graph or chart to represent the data effectively.

Write persuasive statements about the data to support what you want to change.

Present the project.

Probability

Let's investigate

What is the chance of spinning a '3' on the hexagonal spinner?

What is the chance of spinning a '6' on the pentagonal spinner?

What is the chance of spinning a '2' on the hexagonal spinner?

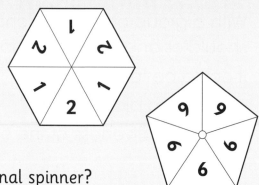

Vocabulary

chance: the likelihood that a particular outcome will occur.

probability: the chance that a particular outcome will occur, considering the total possible outcomes.

likelihood: the chance that a particular outcome will occur.

impossible: an event has no chance of occurring, it has a probability of 0.

certain: an event that will definitely occur, it has a probability of 1.

likely: an event that will probably happen, it has a probability between $\frac{1}{2}$ and 1.

unlikely: an event that will probably not happen, it has a probability between 0 and $\frac{1}{2}$.

evens: an event where there is the same chance of it occurring as not occurring, it has a probability of $\frac{1}{2}$.

equally likely: when the chance of different outcomes is the same, for example, what number will show when you roll a dice.

Asteroid could hit Earth in 2036

A 100-metre wide asteroid will brush past the Earth at a distance of 30 000 km. There is little chance of it hitting us now, but a 'tiny but real' likelihood that it may hit us in 2036.

Road accident risk doubles when children are 11 and 12 years old

Research suggest that the risk of being injured or killed on the roads rises at the point when children who had previously been accompanied to and from school begin to make their own way there and back.

High Probability that Paris will have a White Christmas

After mild temperatures for most of the month, Paris finally saw some snow this week. Right now forecasts predict a white Christmas, although just how white is still uncertain.

'100% chance' of global recession

There are big threats lurking on the horizon to which the world is turning a blind eye. There is a good chance that it will turn into outright recession.

How to avoid flu from your phone

Experts say that mobile phones are 10 times as dirty as a toilet seat! Flu, however, is rarely carried on your phone. The real problem is germs on your hands. Doctors advise reducing the risk of catching flu by washing your hands before touching your phone.

New School Deadline 'unlikely' but 'not impossible'

An expert has said the two-year timeframe for the completion of a proposed new school is "very unlikely, but not impossible". He said, "A build of this sort would normally take up to three years."

1   Read the newspaper articles.
    Write down the words in the articles that are used to describe probability.

2   Draw a probability line from 'impossible' to 'certain'.
    Mark on the line the probability of these events happening,
    according to the newspaper articles:

    • Chance that the new school will be completed on time.
    • Chance of the asteroid hitting Earth in 2036.
    • Chance of a global recession.
    • Chance that Paris will have a white Christmas.

3   Complete the speech bubbles for each person
    using the information from the newspaper articles.

I read that it is less likely for ... to happen than ...

It says that ... is more likely to happen than ...

4 Manuel is keen to have a blue marble so he can win a prize.
   He can choose one bag and then must close his eyes and
   take a marble from the bag he has chosen.

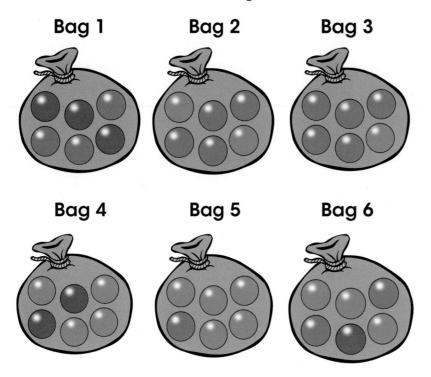

Bag 1   **Bag 2**   **Bag 3**

Bag 4   **Bag 5**   **Bag 6**

(a) Which bag gives him the best chance of taking a blue marble?

(b) Which bag has an even chance of getting a red or blue marble?

(c) Which bag is he least likely to take a blue marble from?

(d) Which bag is it certain that he will not get a green marble from?

(e) Which bag has the greatest chance of taking a green marble?

Is it fair?

This is a game to play with a partner. Try to find out if it is a fair game.

Player One take three red counters or cubes, and one yellow counter or cube.

Player Two take five red counters or cubes, and two yellow counters or cubes.

Put the counters or cubes into a bag, an envelope, or under a book so that you can take them out randomly.

1   Discuss which player you think is most likely to pull a red counter/ cube out of their bag. Finish this sentence to write down your prediction:

I think Player _____ is more likely to pull out a red cube than Player

_____ because _____ .

2   Both players start at 'start'.

Both players take a random cube from their bag. If the cube is red they move forward one space. Replace the cube in the bag.

Keep pulling cubes out of the bag until one player reaches 'finish'.

The player reaching the 'finish' first is the winner.

3   Does playing this game change what you think about the probability of pulling a red cube out of each of the bags? Explain why.

4   Share the results of your game with other pairs of learners. Find out if they got the same results.

Number

The number system (2)

Let's investigate

Use these four cards.

Make as many numbers as possible between 0 and 40.

You must use all four cards each time.

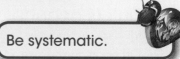

Be systematic.

1   Place these numbers in order of size starting with the smallest.
   (a) 7.3   3.7   0.37   7.03   3.03
   (b) 450 450   54 045   54 405   450 005   450 405

2   Use < and > to show the relationship between these pairs of numbers
   (a) 7.34 and 7.43   (b) 1.23 and 1.2
   (c) 0.34 and 0.05   (d) 1.78 and 1.9

3   The tallest structure in the world is the Burj Khalifa in Dubai.
   It is 829.84 metres high.
   What is this height to the nearest whole number?

4   Haibo put a number in her calculator. She multiplies the number by 10 and the calculator shows:

   $$1.23$$

   What number did Haibo put in the calculator?

5   Write the number that is three ones, four tenths and five hundredths.

6   In the number 65.43 which digit is in the tenths place?

7 Which of these four numbers rounds to 190 000 to the nearest thousand?

185 809   189 099   189 599   191 099

8 Arrange these numbers in order of size starting with the smallest.

613 082   231 068   213 608   613 820

9 What is the missing number?

28.13 = 28 + **?** + 0.03

10 Write the number eighty eight thousand and eight in figures.

11 What is the missing number in this sequence?

700 090, [   ] ,   698 090,   697 090 . . .

12 Saeed has these cards.

(a) Make the largest possible number using these cards.

(b) Make the smallest possible number using these cards.

The decimal point must be between two of the number cards.

13 What is the sum of 500 thousands and 50 tens?

14 What is 20.05 kilometres in metres?

15 Here are four numbers.

123.63   123.69   123.65   123.64

Which of these numbers is 123.6 when rounded to 1 decimal place?

16 Round 9583 to the nearest ten.

17 Which decimal is represented by the arrow on the number line?

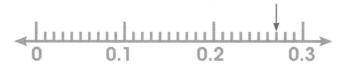

0   0.1   0.2   0.3

18 Which of the following numbers is closest to 0.1?

0.9   0.2   0.11   0.05   0.01

Mental strategies for addition and subtraction (2)

Let's investigate

Use the numbers 1 to 8 so that each side of the square adds up to 15.

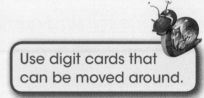

Use digit cards that can be moved around.

1   Write the numbers 1, 2, 3, 4, 5, 6 and 7 in the circles so that each line adds up to 12.

Use each number only once.

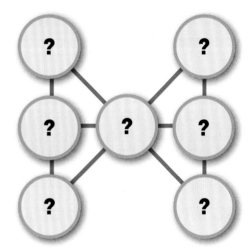

2   Use the numbers 1, 2, 3, 4 and 5 to complete this star pattern. All lines of numbers must add up to 24.

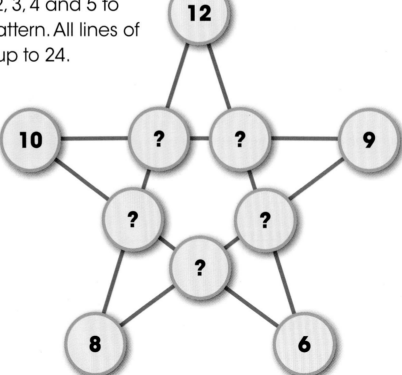

Mental strategies for multiplication and division

Let's investigate

Replace each symbol with a digit to make the division correct.

$$\square\,)\,\overline{\square\,\bigcirc\cdot\square}^{\,\triangle\,\square\cdot\triangle}$$

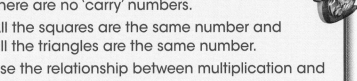

1 There are no 'carry' numbers.
2 All the squares are the same number and all the triangles are the same number.
3 Use the relationship between multiplication and division to help you.

Answer these questions mentally as quickly as you can.

1 Calculate 1.3 multiplied by 4.

2 Divide 4.2 by 6.

3 Divide 3.5 by 10.

4 Double 15.5.

5 What is 10.5 divided by 5?

6 Multiply 3.5 by 4.

7 What is half of 1.6?

8 What is the product of 7 and 0.6?

9 Divide 7.5 by 3.

10 What is double 1.8?

11 Find the missing numbers.
   (a) $0.7 \times 9 =$?   (b) $0.7 \times 8 =$?   (c) $0.7 \times 5 =$?
   (d) $0.2 \times$? $= 1.8$ (e) ? $\times 9 = 5.4$ (f) ? $\times 6 = 4.2$

12 Find the missing numbers.
   (a) $7.2 \div 6 =$?   (b) $4.8 \div 8 =$?   (c) $8.1 \div$? $= 0.9$
   (d) $3.6 \div$? $= 0.4$ (e) ? $\div 7 = 0.2$ (f) ? $\div 6 = 0.8$

Addition and subtraction

Let's investigate

Arrange the digits 0, 1, 2, 3, 4, 5, 6 and 7 to make two numbers with two decimal places so that:

(a) the sum of the numbers is as close as possible to 40

(b) the difference between the numbers is as close as possible to 10.

The zero must not be placed in the tens or hundredths position.

 and

Use digit cards.

1 For each pair of numbers find:

(i) the larger number

(ii) the difference between the numbers.

      (a) −5 and −1   (b) −4 and −6   (c) −9 and −2

      (d) −5 and 4   (e) −2 and −12 (f) 0 and −6

2 Complete these calculations.

    (a) 14.8 + 5.6   (b) 13.26 + 17.64   (c) 45.83 + 31.04

    (d) 56.1 − 26.6   (e) 68.63 − 52.75   (f) 70.34 − 49.78

3 There are three bags for sale in a shop.

    Bag A – $16.50   **Bag B – $13.35**   **Bag C – $11.80**

Mira buys bag B and bag C.

How much did she spend?

4 Find the difference between 15.05 and 14.91.

5 What is the total of $110.21, $5.45 and $17.07?

6 Use these numbers to answer the following questions.

  -5 -4 -3 -2 -1 0 1 2 3 4 5

  (a) Which two numbers have a difference of 8?

  (b) Which two numbers have a difference of 4?

7 Anton and Cheng each buy a book.
Cheng pays with a $10 note and gets
$1.05 change.
Anton's book costs $6.79.
How much more does Cheng pay for
his book than Anton?

8 Copy and complete the diagram
so that the three numbers in each
line add up to 10.

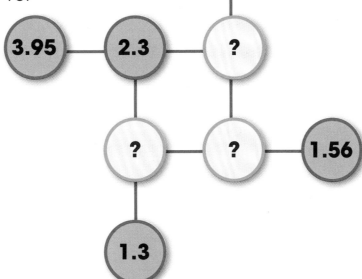

9 Find the missing digits to make these calculations correct.

```
    8 · ? 7              ? 1 · 3 ?
 -  ? · 6 ?           -  1 ? · ? 1
 ──────────          ────────────
    3 · 6 9             1 4 · 9 8
```

The laws of arithmetic

Let's investigate

Use any of the numbers 1, 2, 3 and 4 together with brackets and the operation signs to make as many numbers from 11 to 20 as you can.

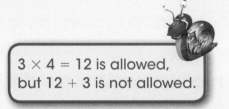

3 × 4 = 12 is allowed, but 12 + 3 is not allowed.

How many numbers can you make using 1, 2, 3 and 4 in the calculation?

This is an example of using all four numbers:
(4 + 2) × (3 − 1) = 16

The order of operations is important in daily life.

Which do you do first, catch the school bus or wake up?

Remember: brackets first!

1   Work out the answers to the following:
   (a) (3 × 4) + 6 = **?**   (b) 7 + (11 − 6) = **?**
   (c) (14 ÷ 7) + 13 = **?**   (d) (2 + 3) − (4 − 1) = **?**
   (e) (14 − 6) × (3 + 1) = **?**   (f) (27 ÷ 9) × 4 = **?**

2   Are the following statements true or false?
    Explain your decisions to your partner.
   (a) (3 + 6) × 2 = 3 + (6 × 2)
   (b) 6 + (8 ÷ 2) = 6 + 8 ÷ 2
   (c) (7 − 2) × 3 = 7 − (2 × 3)
   (d) (3 × 4) × 5 = 3 × (4 × 5)
   (e) 5 × 3 − 5 = (5 × 3) − 5

3   Put brackets in these calculations to make them correct.
    (a) $6 + 2 \times 5 = 40$ (b) $3 + 4 \times 2 + 4 = 42$
    (c) $3 \times 4 + 2 = 18$ (d) $4 + 3 + 2 \times 2 = 18$

4   Are the following statements true or false? If the statement is false,
    write it out correctly.
    (a) $9 \times 4 = 36$
    (b) $6 + 3 \times 4 = 18$
    (c) $(6 + 3) \times 4 = 36$
    (d) $(6 + 3) \times 4 = 18$

> multiplication and
> division before addition
> and subtraction!

5   Write the answers to these calculations
    (a) $7 + 2 \times 4 =$ **?**   (b) $5 \times 8 - 4 =$ **?**
    (c) $15 + 20 \div 5 =$ **?**   (d) $17 - 6 \times 2 =$ **?**
    (e) $18 - 16 \div 4 =$ **?**   (f) $4 \times 6 - 3 \times 5 =$ **?**

6   Use these numbers together with brackets and operation signs to make
    the target number.
    (a) 2, 5 and 5 to give 35
    (b) 5, 7 and 10 to give 120
    (c) 2, 5 and 14 to give 18

> **Remember:** 5×42
> We can use $= 5 \times (40 + 2)$
> brackets to show $= (5 \times 40) + (5 \times 2)$
> stages in thought $= 200 + 10$
> processess. $= 210$

7   Calculate
    (a) 4×71 (b) 6×45 (c) 4×74 (d) 9×16
    (e) 5×68 (f) 7×68 (g) 3×93 (h) 8×73

8   Find the missing numbers
    (a) $(3 \times 4) +$ **?** $= 19$ (b) $(5 \times 5) -$ **?** $= 23$
    (c) $(4 \times 5) -$ **?** $= 12$

9   Write the correct sign <, > or = to make these statements correct
    (a) $(8 + 5) - 7$ **?** $(8 + 7) - 5$
    (b) $2 \times (3 + 4)$ **?** $(2 \times 3) + 4$
    (c) $(10 \times 5) \div 2$ **?** $10 \times (5 \div 2)$

Fractions and division

Let's investigate

Find all the calculations that have an answer of 10.

$\frac{2}{3}$ of 15	$\frac{50}{5}$	$\frac{1}{2}$ of 20	$\frac{3}{4}$ of 20
$\frac{20}{2}$	$30 \div 3$	$60 \div 4$	$\frac{45}{3}$
$\frac{1}{3}$ of 45	$45 \div 5$	$\frac{60}{4}$	$20 \div 2$
$50 \div 5$	$\frac{1}{3}$ of 30	$\frac{1}{4}$ of 60	$\frac{1}{5}$ of 50

1   Work out the calculations. Give your answer as a mixed number.

    (a) $227 \div 4$ **(b)** $429 \div 7$ **(c)** $525 \div 9$

    (d) $389 \div 5$ **(e)** $315 \div 6$ **(f)** $459 \div 8$

2   Work out the calculations. Give your answer as a decimal.

    (a) $491 \div 4$ **(b)** $375 \div 2$ **(c)** $468 \div 5$

3   Answer these questions mentally.

    (a) How many forties are there in four hundred?

    (b) What is two thirds of ninety nine?

    (c) Four times a number is four hundred. What is the number?

    (d) What is the remainder when 28 is divided by five?

    (e) Six times a number is three thousand. What is the number?

    (f) What is one fifth of a thousand?

    (g) When a number is divided by seven, the answer is two, remainder two. What is the number?

    (h) What is three quarters of forty four?

    (i) Halve twenty five.

    (j) Divide five hundred by twenty five.

4   Calculate.

    (a) $630 \div 14$ **(b)** $782 \div 17$ **(c)** $777 \div 21$

    (d) $855 \div 19$ **(e)** $696 \div 12$ **(f)** $858 \div 22$

5   Find

(a) $\frac{2}{3}$ of 24   (b) $\frac{3}{5}$ of 30   (c) $\frac{7}{10}$ of 70

(d) $\frac{3}{10}$ of 30   (e) $\frac{17}{100}$ of 500   (f) $\frac{9}{10}$ of 180

6   Which is larger: $\frac{7}{10}$ of $90 or $\frac{3}{5}$ of $100?

7   Wafa makes a pattern on a square grid.

She colours $\frac{1}{4}$ of the squares blue.

She colours $\frac{1}{2}$ of the squares red.

She colours the other squares green.
How many squares are green?

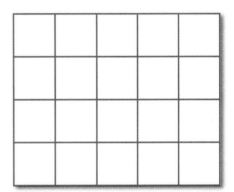

8   Here are five numbers.

$4\frac{6}{10}$ 4.6 $4\frac{3}{10}$ $4\frac{3}{5}$ 4.3

Which of these numbers is the result of dividing 23 by 5?

9   Cheng bought some books in a sale.

Sale price: $\frac{1}{5}$ off

The original price was $80.
How much did Cheng pay for the books?

Fractions

Let's investigate

"All fractions that are equivalent to $\frac{1}{2}$ have a denominator that is an even number."

Investigate whether this statement is correct?

Write about your findings.

Vocabulary

equivalent fractions: are equal in value. For example,

$$\frac{3}{5} \overset{\times 2}{\underset{\times 2}{=}} \frac{6}{10}$$

cancel or simplify: means to reduce the numerator and denominator of a fraction to the smallest numbers possible.

For example, $\frac{4}{12} \rightarrow \frac{1}{2}$

1   Complete the equivalent fractions in these spider diagrams.

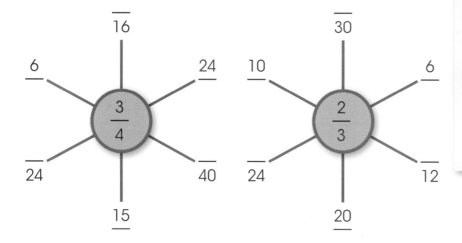

2   Simplify these fractions by cancelling.

(a) $\frac{14}{21} = \frac{2}{?}$ (b) $\frac{6}{30} = \frac{?}{5}$ (c) $\frac{24}{36} = \frac{2}{?}$

(d) $\frac{15}{20} = \frac{?}{4}$ (e) $\frac{15}{25} = \frac{3}{?}$ (f) $\frac{12}{16} = \frac{?}{4}$

3   Write these fractions in the simplest form.

(a) $\frac{14}{28}$ (b) $\frac{9}{36}$ (c) $\frac{15}{45}$ (d) $\frac{9}{15}$

4 Maria makes a fraction using two number cards.

She says my fraction is equivalent to half.

One of her numbers is 10. What could
Maria's fraction be?

Is there more than one possible answer?

5 Copy these grids and shade in these fractions.

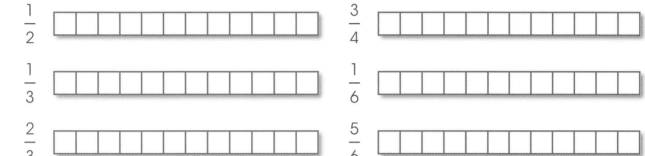

$\dfrac{1}{2}$

$\dfrac{3}{4}$

$\dfrac{1}{3}$

$\dfrac{1}{6}$

$\dfrac{2}{3}$

$\dfrac{5}{6}$

$\dfrac{1}{4}$

Use your results to help you answer these questions.

(a) Find the correct sign $<$, $>$ or $=$ to make each statement correct.

(i) $\dfrac{1}{4}$ **?** $\dfrac{1}{3}$

(ii) $\dfrac{2}{3}$ **?** $\dfrac{5}{6}$

(iii) $\dfrac{5}{12}$ **?** $\dfrac{1}{3}$

(iv) $\dfrac{11}{12}$ **?** $\dfrac{5}{6}$

(v) $\dfrac{9}{12}$ **?** $\dfrac{3}{4}$

(vi) $\dfrac{1}{6}$ **?** $\dfrac{1}{3}$

(b) Write these fractions in order starting with the smallest.

(i) $\dfrac{1}{2}$ $\dfrac{1}{3}$ $\dfrac{5}{12}$ $\dfrac{1}{6}$

(ii) $\dfrac{2}{3}$ $\dfrac{4}{12}$ $\dfrac{5}{6}$ $\dfrac{1}{2}$

6 Anton scores 5 out of 10 in a test.

Flavia scores 10 out of 20 in a different test.

Who achieves the better result?

Explain how you know.

Mixed numbers and improper fractions

Let's investigate

Roll two 1–6 dice and use them to make an improper fraction. If you roll a 'double' you will have a whole number.

Change the improper fractions to mixed numbers.

Investigate how many different mixed numbers can be made.

Be systematic.

1   Change each improper fraction to a mixed number.

(a) $\frac{13}{4}$ (b) $\frac{7}{30}$ (c) $\frac{11}{5}$

(d) $\frac{9}{7}$ (e) $\frac{11}{8}$ (f) $\frac{5}{3}$

2   Change each mixed number to an improper fraction.

(a) $1\frac{1}{4}$ (b) $2\frac{1}{3}$ (c) $3\frac{2}{3}$ (d) $4\frac{2}{5}$ (e) $5\frac{2}{3}$ (f) $4\frac{1}{6}$

3   Four pizzas are each cut into quarters.
   (a) How many pieces are cut?
   (b) Five pieces are eaten. How much pizza is left?

   Write your answer as an improper fraction and a mixed number.

4   What are the two missing mixed numbers on this number line?

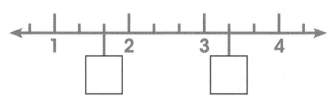

Fractions and decimals

Let's investigate

Kiki says 10.7 is equivalent to $\frac{7}{10}$.

Davy says it should be 0.7 and Mohammed says it should be 1.07.

Do you agree with any of these students?

Draw a picture to help explain why.

1 Convert these fractions to decimals.

(a) $\frac{1}{10}$ (b) $\frac{1}{2}$ (c) $\frac{2}{5}$ (d) $\frac{3}{5}$

(e) $\frac{3}{4}$ (f) $\frac{3}{8}$ (g) $\frac{4}{5}$ (h) $\frac{5}{8}$

2 Ahmed has the digit cards 0, 1, 2 and 5.
Arrange the digit cards to make this correct

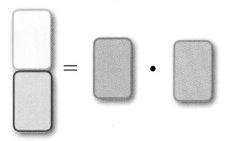

3 Which number is the greater $\frac{1}{4}$ or 0.4?
Explain how you know.

4 Look at this grid.

0.3	$\frac{7}{10}$	$\frac{1}{2}$	0.8
0.6	$\frac{2}{5}$	0.2	$\frac{1}{10}$

Which number satisfies all the criteria:

The fraction is less than $\frac{1}{2}$ The fraction is not equal to $\frac{3}{10}$

The fraction is greater than 0.1   The fraction is not equal to $\frac{1}{5}$

Percentages

Let's investigate

A wealthy farmer has four sons and a 3-section farm as shown in the diagram.

The farmer wants to give his farm to his sons so that each receives 25%. But he says that each son must have a farm the same shape as the original.

How is the farm divided?

Divide the three sections into squares.

The orientation of the sons' farms does not have to be the same.

1   Copy and complete the table showing equivalent fractions and percentages.

	Fraction	Percentage
(a)	$\frac{63}{100}$	
(b)		40%
(c)	$\frac{1}{4}$	
(d)		10%
(e)	$\frac{9}{100}$	

2   Find each percentage. Start by finding 10% of each amount.
   (a) 10% of 50 = ?   so 20% of 50 = ?
   (b) 10% of $70 = ?   so 30% of $70 = ?
   (c) 10% of 750 mm = ?   so 70% of 750 mm = ?
   (d) 10% of 40 cm = ?   so 5% of 40 cm = ?

3 (a) What is 50% of 40?

  (b) What is 99% of 200?

  (c) What is 3% of 300?

4 (a) What is 20% of 90 metres?

  (b) What is 20 out of 40 as a percentage?

5 A bicycle is priced at $250.
  It is marked 30% off.
  What is the new price?

6 Find the missing numbers.

  (a) 30% of 60 is ? .

  (b) 30% of ? is 60.

7 A bottle of water contains 500 ml.
  A larger bottle holds 30% more.
  How much does the larger bottle hold?

8 10% of a number is 13. What is the number?

9 Write the symbols >, < or = in the boxes to make each statement true.

  (a) 10% ? $\frac{1}{10}$

  (b) 20% of $10 ? $2.50

  (c) 3 out of 4 ? 70%

10% of my number is 6

10 Fatima is thinking of a number.
   She says:
   What number is Fatima thinking of?

11 Bruno says
   30% of 50 is smaller than 50% of 30
   Is Bruno right? Explain your answer.

Ratio and proportion

Let's investigate

Caleb has two litres of red paint and three litres of yellow paint. The orange he wants to make is called *Glorious Sunrise*.

Glorious Sunrise needs a ratio of two amounts of yellow for every one amount of red (2 : 1).

How many litres of *Glorious Sunrise* can Caleb make with his red and yellow paint?

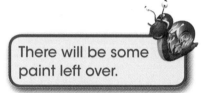

There will be some paint left over.

1 These tile patterns should all have a ratio of three red tiles for every two yellow tiles (3 : 2).

(a) What should be the colour of the missing tile in each pattern?

(i)

Write the proportion as a fraction.

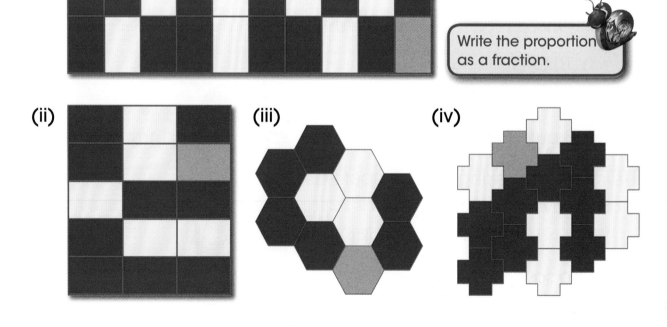

(ii)   (iii)   (iv)

(b) What proportion of the tiles in these patterns should be red?

(c) What proportion of the tiles in these patterns should be yellow?

2   Here is a pocketful of coins that are used in Australia.

(a) What is the ratio of bronze to silver coins in this group?

(b) What proportion of the coins in the group has a value of more than 15 cents?

(c) What is the ratio of round to not round coins in the group?

(d) What proportion of the coins has a value of less than 8 cents?

(e) What proportion of the coins has a value of 20 cents?

3 Read what each child is saying and work out if it is true or false:

(a)

Sweet Pink paint is mixed so that there is one part of red paint to every five parts of white paint. In 1.2 litres of *Sweet Pink* 1 litre is white paint.

(b)

In my jar of marbles three eighths of the marbles are red. If I have 24 marbles in the jar, then 16 of them must not be red.

(c)

The ratio 3:4 is the same as the proportion $\frac{3}{4}$.

(d)

The ratio 3:4 is the same as the proportion $\frac{3}{7}$.

(e)

We won the netball match by 5 goals to 3. $\frac{5}{8}$ of the goals were scored by us.

(f)

At the school fair the ratio of adults to children was 2:5. There were 280 people and 180 of them were children.

(g)

There are 27 children in our class. 24 of us like strawberries. $\frac{1}{9}$ of us do not like strawberries.

4 Here is the menu board for the milkshake shop.

Milkshake menu

First we blend delicious vanilla ice cream and milk.

Then choose from these flavours:

Beenuts! (peanut sauce and honey mixed 3:2)

Chocomint! (peppermint syrup & chocolate syrup mixed 1:2)

Orange Chocolate! (chocolate syrup & orange juice mixed 1:4)

Cranberry Wish! (cranberry juice & orange juice mixed 5:2)

Apple Honey! (apple juice & honey mixed 3:1)

(a) If 20 ml of chocolate syrup is used to make one Chocomint milkshake.
How much peppermint syrup is needed?

(b) A Beenuts! milkshake needs 60 ml of peanut sauce. How much honey would be needed to make three Beenuts! milkshakes?

(c) A new milkshake called Apple Crunch uses 120 ml of apple juice and 80 ml of peanut sauce. How should the ratio be written on the menu board?

(d) If a Cranberry Wish milkshake needs 40 ml of orange juice, how many milkshakes can be made with 1 litre of orange juice?

How much cranberry juice would be needed for that many milkshakes?

Measure

Metric and imperial measures (1)

Let's investigate

Kabir has three fuel containers. One holds 7 gallons, one holds 4 gallons and one holds 3 gallons. Only the 7 gallon container is full, the others are empty.

What is the quickest way to transfer the fuel so that two of the containers contain 2 gallons each, and the third contains 3 gallons?

Vocabulary

gallon: an imperial measure of capacity or liquid volume.

quart: an imperial measure of capacity or liquid volume, there are four quarts in a gallon.

pint: an imperial measure of capacity or liquid volume, there are two pints in a quart.

pounds: an imperial measure of mass.

ounces: an imperial measure of mass, there are 16 ounces in a pound.

Conversion table – Litres to Imperial Pints	
Litres	Imperial Pints
1	1.76
2	3.52
5	8.80
10	17.60

Conversion table – Litres to Imperial Pints	
Imperial Pints	Litres
1	0.568
2	1.137
5	2.841
10	5.683

1   Sally has measured the surface area of the walls in her house so that she can work out how much paint she needs to decorate the rooms. She knows that she will need 8 pints of paint for every 400 square feet of wall, but the paint tins come in litres. What tins should she buy for each of these rooms:

(a) hallway 400 square feet in Lemon Yellow

(b) bathroom 200 square feet in Ice Blue

(c) bedroom 700 square feet in Coral Pink

(d) kitchen 1300 square feet in Lichen Green?

(e) Approximately what area of wall could be painted with five 2 litre tins of paint?

2 This is a line graph showing the conversion between imperial pounds and kilograms.

Use the graph to approximately convert these amounts into pounds, to the nearest $\frac{1}{2}$ of a pound

(a) 5 kg

(b) 8 kg

(c) 4 kg

(d) 6 kg

(e) $2\frac{1}{2}$ kg

3 Use the graph to approximately convert these amounts into kilograms, to the nearest 0.1 kg

(a) 14 lb

(b) $7\frac{3}{4}$ lb

(c) 16 lb

(d) $12\frac{3}{4}$ lb

(e) $1\frac{1}{4}$ lb

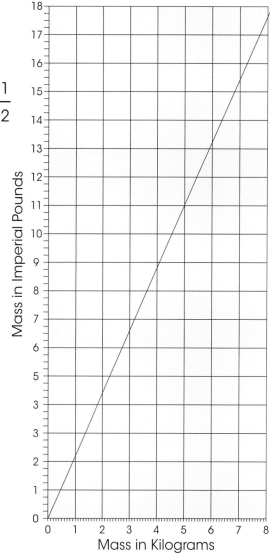

4 Which is better value:

(a) 6 kg of butter for $5 or 13 lb of butter for $5?

(b) 4 kg of butter for $3 or 18 lb of butter for $6?

(c) 7.5 kg of butter for $6 or 25 lb for $9?

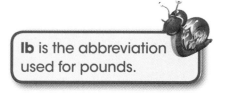

lb is the abbreviation used for pounds.

Metric and imperial measures (2)

Let's investigate

A 6 inch ruler with marks only at 1 inch, 3 inches, and 6 inches can be used to measure 2 inches by using the distance between 1 and 3 inches. It can be used to measure 5 inches using the distance between 1 and 6 inches. Look at the riler below. It only has 0 inches and 12 inches marked.

Using what you know about the 6 inch ruler with only 3 marks on it; what is the fewest number of marks you could put on a 12 inch ruler and still be able to measure every distance from 1 inch to 12 inches?

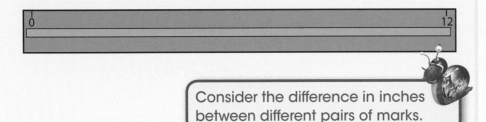

> Consider the difference in inches between different pairs of marks.

This is a ruler that shows inches and centimetres.

1   This is Harvey, an inch worm!

He is 2 inches long and $\frac{1}{2}$ inch wide.

Draw the other members of his family:

(a) baby sister, 1 inch long, $\frac{1}{2}$ inch wide

(b) older brother, $3\frac{1}{2}$ inches long, 1 inch wide

(c) parent, 4 inches long, $1\frac{1}{2}$ inches wide

(d) parent 5 inches long, 2 inches wide.

2 Put these lengths in order of size, smallest to greatest.

$2\frac{1}{2}$ inches

$1\frac{1}{2}$ inches

6.5 cm

58 mm

2.85 cm

5.58 cm

3 The map shows the course for a new European car rally, starting in Paris and finishing in Berlin. The car rally tests drivers' navigational and driving skills.

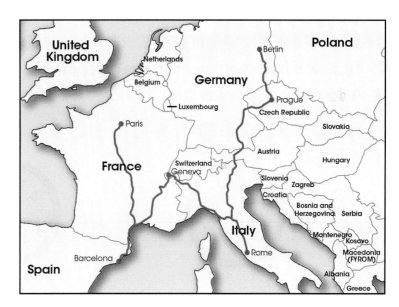

This table shows the distances between each city on the route in kilometres.

Barcelona					
1880 km	**Berlin**				
785 km	1119 km	**Geneva**			
1038 km	1053 km	541 km	**Paris**		
1721 km	351 km	973 km	1031 km	**Prague**	
1359 km	1510 km	880 km	1414 km	1304 km	**Rome**

(a) Which order are the cities visited on the rally?

(b) How far is it from Barcelona to Geneva in Kilometres?

(b) How far is it from Barcelona to Geneva in miles?

(d) Approximately how many miles in total is the complete rally?

(e) Choose a different route for the rally, visiting each of the cities marked on the map. Work out the distance of your rally in km and in miles.

1 kilometre = 0.62 miles

Multiply the number of kilometres by 0.62 to convert to miles.

1 mile = 1.6 kilometres

Multiply the number of miles by 1.6 to convert to kilometres.

Time zones (2)

Let's investigate

These children have different birth months, but were all born in the same year before May. Find out who was born in each month.

1 Meena was born before Jess.

2 Jess was born two months after Adam.

3 Adam was born after Josh but before Meena.

Vocabulary

time zones: regions on the earth surface that share a common time.

You could write the names on separate pieces of paper and then rearrange them against the months until all three statements are true.

1
Lima (05:51)

Sao Paulo (07:51)

Cape Town (12:51)

Karachi (15:21)

Tokyo (19:51)

Adelaide (20:21)

This is a table to show the time difference between cities. The table shows that there is a 14 hour time difference between Lima and Tokyo.

Lima						
	Sao Paulo					
		Cape Town				
			Karachi			
14 hours				Tokyo		
					Adelaide	

Copy and complete this table showing the time difference between the different cities using the clocks above.

2   Use your table from question 1 to help you calculate the day and time in :

(a) Cape Town if it is 08:13 on Wednesday in Lima

(b) Karachi if it is 10:37 pm on Saturday in Cape Town

(c) Sao Paulo if it is 17:28 on Tuesday in Tokyo

(d) Lima if it is 9:09 am on Friday in Adelaide.

3   This is a Flight Timetable. Use the information in the timetable (and the time differences) to work out the length of time, in hours and minutes, of each journey (a) to (e).

	Departure city	Destination city	Departure time at departure city	Arrival time at destination city
(a)	Lima	Sao Paulo	13:45 (Mon)	20:35 (Mon)
(b)	Adelaide	Tokyo	17:35 (Weds)	06:05 (Thurs)
(c)	Sao Paulo	Karachi	01:25 (Tues)	04:30 (Weds)
(d)	Cape Town	Adelaide	18:05 (Fri)	22:25 (Sat)
(e)	Adelaide	Lima	09:30 (Sat)	00:20 (Sun)

First work out what the time is in the **arrival city** at the time when the plane leaves the departure city, and then work out the time interval between this time and the arrival time.

For example, for part (a) you need to calculate how long the journey is from Lima to Sao Paulo. The departure time in Lima is 13:45, so the time in Sao Paulo at that time would be 15:45 because it is 2 hours ahead of Lima. Draw a time line:

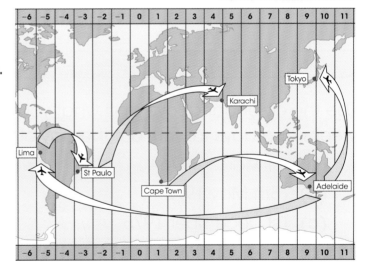

So the journey takes 4 hours and 50 minutes.

(f) Dawn flew from Cape Town to Adelaide, then Adelaide to Tokyo. How long did she spend travelling?

(g) Patrick flew from Adelaide to Lima, then from Lima to Sao Paulo, then Sao Paulo to Karachi. How long did he spend travelling?

It's a date

Below is a page from the calendar for 1976.

January 1976						
Monday	**Tuesday**	**Wednesday**	**Thursday**	**Friday**	**Saturday**	**Sunday**
–	–	–	1	2	3	4
5	6	7	8	9	10	11
12	13	14	15	16	17	18
19	20	21	22	23	24	25
26	27	28	29	30	31	–

Use the calendar above and what you know about years, months, weeks and days to work out the day of the week of on:

(a) 1st March 1976

(b) 15th May 1976

(c) 1st December 1975

(d) 22nd July 1976

(e) 31st December 1976

(f) 1st March 1977

Remember to work out whether the year is a leap year.

Area and perimeter of rectangles

Let's investigate

Tia says:

I can double the area of a rectangle by doubling the length and doubling the width.

Is Tia correct? Explain your answer.

1   What is the area and perimeter of the front covers of these magazines?

(a)

28 cm

20 cm

(b)

28 cm

13 cm

(c)

10 cm

16.5 cm

(d)

9.7 cm

19 cm

(e)

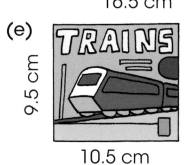

9.5 cm

10.5 cm

2 Draw the rectangles listed in the table and work out their area and perimeter.

	length	width	area	perimeter
(a)	7 cm	4 cm		
(b)	5.5 cm	3 cm		
(c)	8 cm	5.2 cm		
(d)	6.7 cm	5 cm		
(e)	4.5 cm	2.5 cm		

3 To work out the area of a rectangle multiply its length by its width. We can write this as:

length × width = area or $l \times w = a$

Write and complete the following:

(a) width × ___ = area

(b) area ÷ width = ___

(c) area ÷ length = ___

4 Use your answers from question 3 to work out the length of a rectangle with :

(a) a width of 4 cm and an area of 24 cm

(b) a width of 7 cm and an area of 56 cm

(c) a width of 2.5 cm and an area of 25 cm

(d) a width of 1.5 cm and an area of 12 cm

(e) a width of 2.1cm and an area of 16.8 cm

(f) a width of 5 cm and an area of 26 cm.

5 (a) Investigate what size rectangle would have an area of 27.5 cm^2 and a perimeter of 21 cm.

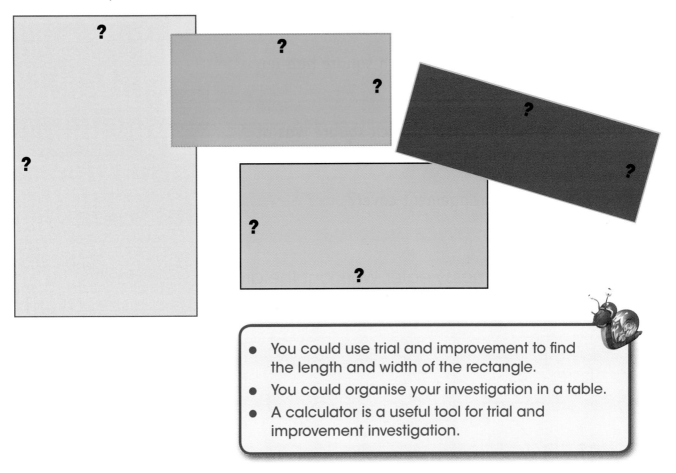

- You could use trial and improvement to find the length and width of the rectangle.
- You could organise your investigation in a table.
- A calculator is a useful tool for trial and improvement investigation.

(b) Draw a rectangle with an area of 27.5 cm^2 and a perimeter of 21 cm. Label the rectangle with its length and width.

Area and perimeter of irregular shapes

Let's investigate

David took two paper squares. Each square had an area of 4 cm².

He arranged so that a corner of each square was at the centre of the other square, like this:

What area does the arrangement cover?

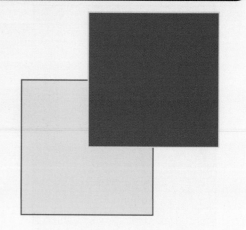

1 Baby Jamie is a messy eater. Work out the area of each stain on his bib. (This is a square centimetre grid.)

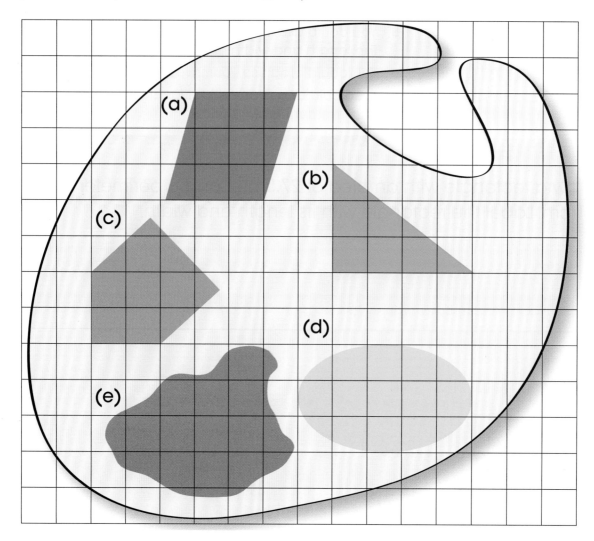

2 Use centimetre square paper to shade six different shapes, that are not rectangular, with an area of approximately 12 cm². Here are some examples:

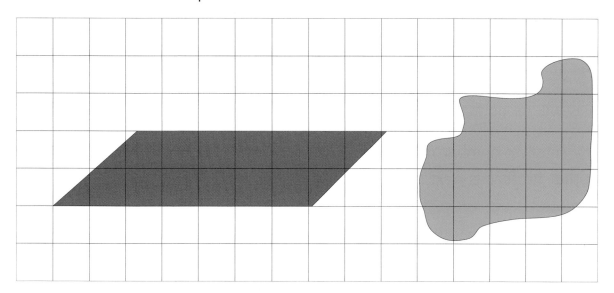

3 Selena made this pattern by overlapping tissue paper triangles.

Below are the bottom three triangles, as they look on a centimetre square grid.

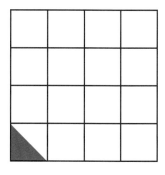
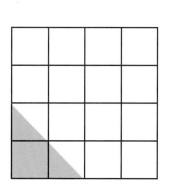
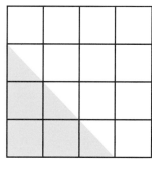

(a) Draw and complete a table to show the area and perimeter of each triangle in the pattern.

(b) What would be the area of the 7th triangle?

(c) What would be the area of the 10th triangle?

Geometry

Quadrilateral prisms and pyramids

Let's investigate

This cube is going to be painted.

Whole faces will be painted in one colour.

What is the smallest number of colours needed so that no face is next to a face of the same colour?

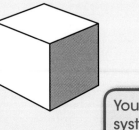

You could try working systematically, e.g. can it be done with 1, 2, 3 colours?

1   Copy this sorting diagram.

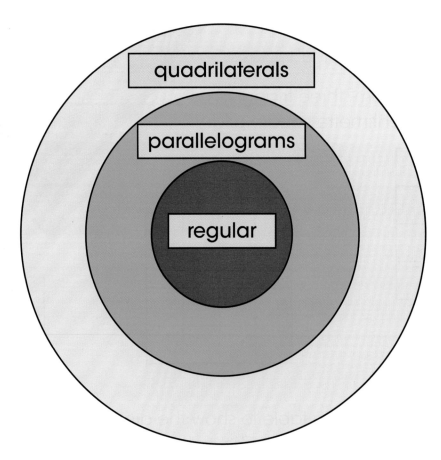

Write these shape names into the correct sections of your diagram.

kite   **rectangle**   **pentagon**   **trapezium**   **square**   **rhombus**

2 **(a)** Copy and complete the table:

Name of shape	Number of faces	Numbers of edges	Number of vertices
Triangle-based pyramid			
Square-based pyramid			
Pentagon-based pyramid			
Hexagon-based pyramid			
Heptagon-based pyramid			
Octagon-based pyramid			

(b) Look at the completed table carefully.

Describe any patterns you see in the numbers. Your could use sentences like:

The number of _____ *is always* _____ *the number of* _____ .

(c) Use your description to complete this table with your prediction for a 50-sided shape based pyramid

Name of shape	Number of faces	Numbers of edges	Number of vertices
50-sided shape based pyramid			

3 **(a)** Draw your own table to investigate the relationship between the faces, edges and vertices of different prisms.

(b) Use what you find out to write down the number of faces, edges and vertices you would expect to find on a 50-sided shape based prism.

Platonic solids – extension only

Let's investigate

This tetrahedron is going to be painted. Whole faces will be painted in one colour.

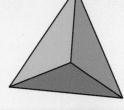

What is the smallest number of colours needed so that no face is next to a face of the same colour?

What about an octahedron?

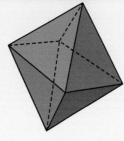

These questions extend understanding beyond Stage 6. Only attempt them if you want a challenge.

1   This is part of a net of a dodecahedron.
    How many pentagons are missing from the net?

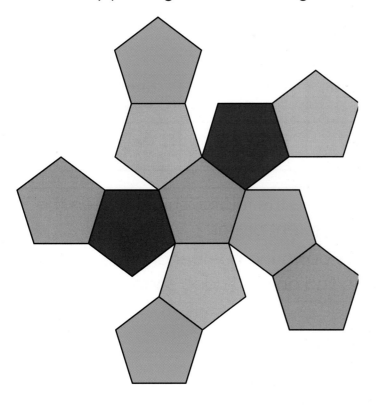

Vocabulary

regular polyhedra: 3D shapes where all faces are the same 2D regular shape.

tetrahedron: a regular 3D shape with four equilateral triangle faces.

cube: a regular 3D shape with six square faces.

octahedron: a regular 3D shape with eight equilateral triangle faces.

icosahedron: a regular 3D shape with 20 equilateral triangular faces.

dodecahedron: a regular 3D shape with 12 pentagonal faces.

2 **(a)** Match the pictures of these polyhedrals to their names.

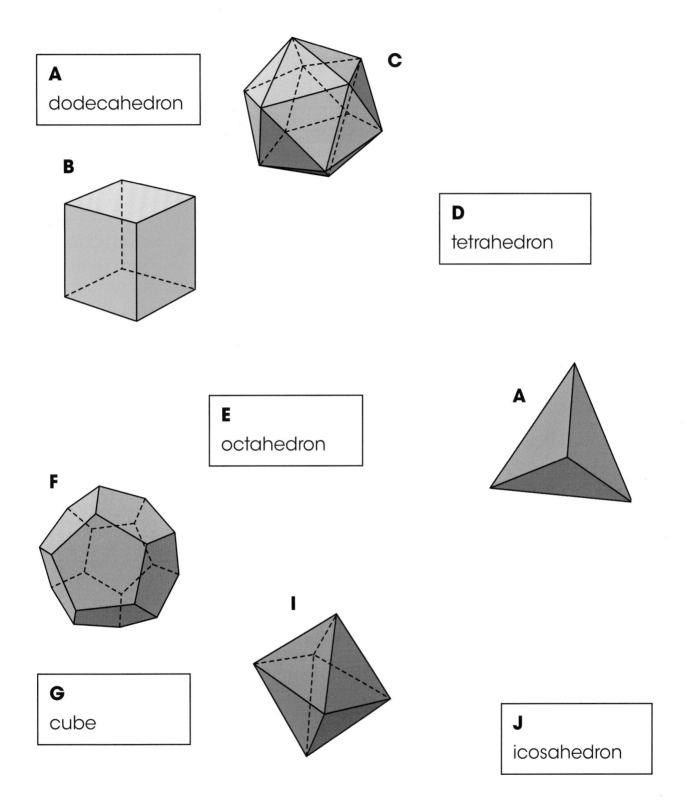

A dodecahedron

B

C

D tetrahedron

E octahedron

A

F

I

G cube

J icosahedron

(b) Explain what is special about this group of polyhedra.

Classifying shapes

Let's investigate

Draw a Venn diagram to classify these shapes into suitable groups.

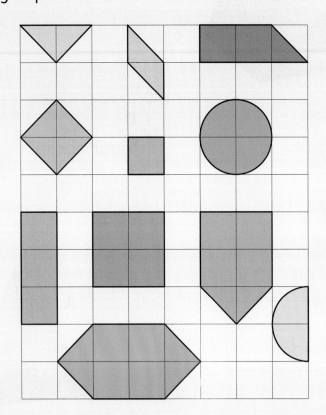

Vocabulary

polygon: a closed 2-dimensional shape having three or more straight sides.

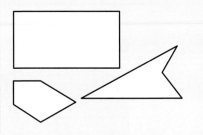

1   **(a)** A square has vertices at (3, 0), (0, 3) and (−3, 0).
        What are the coordinates of the fourth vertex?

    (b) The points (3, 2) and (−1, 2) are two vertices of a square.
        What could the other two vertices be?

    How many solutions can you find?

2   Look at the statements about triangles. For each one, say whether it is possible or impossible.

    • A triangle can have two right angles

    • A triangle can have two acute angles

    • A triangle can have two obtuse angles

3   The grid shows eight different shapes.
    Name each shape.

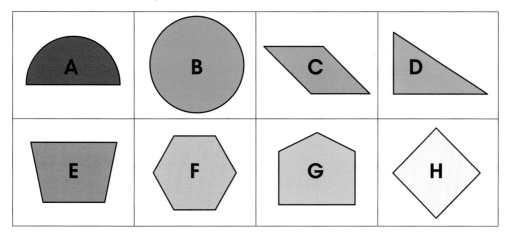

Identify the shape that fits each pair of clues.

(a) It is not a polygon.   (b) It has more than four vertices.
    It has no straight sides.   It is not a regular polygon.

(c) It is a regular polygon.
    It has less than six sides.

4   Sketch the following polygons. Mark the lengths of the sides on
    your diagram. The first one has been done for you.
    Clues

(a) • The polygon has two equal sides.

    • One side of the polygon is double the length of
      another side.

    • The perimeter of the polygon is 40 cm.

(b) • The polygon has four sides.

    • The polygon has four right angles.

    • The length of the polygon is double the width of the polygon.

    • The area of the polygon is 18 cm².

(c) • The polygon has two right angles, the other angles are obtuse.

    • The polygon has five sides.

    • Three of the sides are 4 cm long.

    • The other two sides are shorter than 4 cm.

Transforming shapes

Let's investigate

Frieze patterns

These frieze patterns are formed using reflections, rotations and translations. Investigate patterns in the environment, for example on buildings and in art, or design your own patterns.

1   Draw a triangle on a six by six grid. Reflect it, translate it and rotate it until you have a design you think is attractive or interesting.

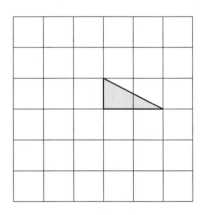

2   A, B, C and D are the vertices of a rectangle. A and B are shown on the grid.

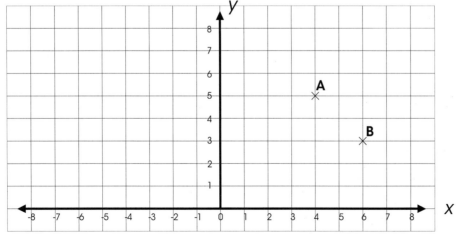

D is the point (3, 4). What are the coordinates of C?

ABCD is reflected in the y-axis. What are the co-ordinates of the image?

Investigating and drawing angles

Let's investigate

Without measuring, work out the angle at X.

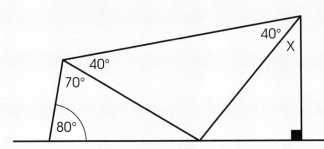

> The sum of the angles on a straight line is 180°.
>
> Work out some of the other missing angles first.

1   An ancient civilization hidden within a distant mountain range, carved their writing into clay tablets as a series of angles. Each size of angle matches a letter in our alphabet or a digit from 0 to 9.

This clay tablet has been smashed. Work out the letter or number on each piece and then rearrange them to discover the word.

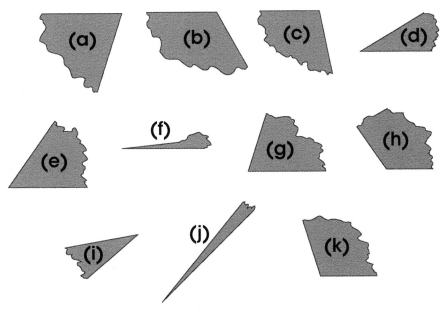

Code			
A	6°	S	114°
B	12°	T	120°
C	18°	U	126°
D	24°	V	132°
E	30°	W	138°
F	36°	X	144°
G	42°	Y	150°
H	48°	Z	156°
I	54°	0	162°
J	60°	1	168°
K	66°	2	174°
L	72°	3	180°
M	78°	4	186°
N	84°	5	194°
O	90°	6	200°
P	96°	7	206°
Q	102°	8	212°
R	108°	9	218°

(l) The word is _____.

2   Draw the angles that would write the word 'triangle'.

3 Four children are making triangles using sticks.

My triangle will have 3 acute angles.

My triangle will have 1 obtuse angle.

My triangle will have 2 obtuse angles.

My triangle will have 2 acute angles.

Can everyone make the triangle they want? Explain your answer.

4 Each of these pies has been cut into unequal slices. Work out the missing angle on each pie, without measuring.

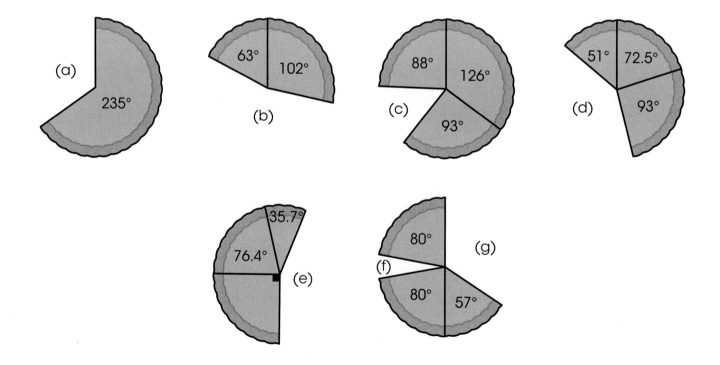

(a) 235°

(b) 63° 102°

(c) 88° 126° 93°

(d) 51° 72.5° 93°

(e) 35.7° 76.4°

(f) 80° 80° 57°

(g)

5 Imagine a pie was cut into **equal** slices. What would be the angle of each piece if it were cut into:

(a) 2 pieces   **(b)** 3 pieces   **(c)** 4 pieces

(d) 5 pieces   **(e)** 6 pieces   **(f)** 7 pieces

(g) 8 pieces   **(h)** 9 pieces   **(i)** 10 pieces

(j) 11 pieces   **(k)** 12 pieces

6 Sebastian drew a triangle. He split the triangle into two right-angled triangles by drawing a dotted line.
Without measuring the angles, work out the angles (a), (b) and (c).

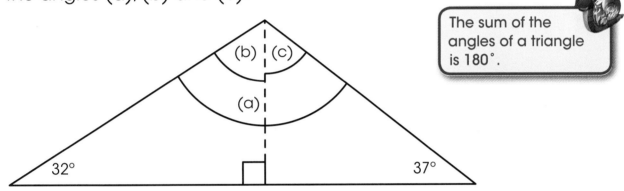

The sum of the angles of a triangle is 180°.

7 Find the angles marked with a shape symbol.

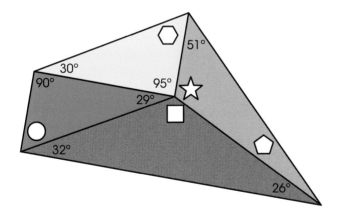

The sum of the angles at a point are 360°.

Work out the angle of some shapes to deduce the other angles.